Learn To Think Using Thought Experiments:

How to Expand Your Mental Horizons, Understand Metacognition, Improve Your Curiosity, and Think Like a Philosopher

By Patrick King
Social Interaction and Conversation Coach at
www.PatrickKingConsulting.com

Table of Contents

Chapter 1. Thinking About Thinking

There was a time when mankind knew so much less about the world. We take so much of what's around us as a given, forgetting where it came from. Look around you and you'll see that almost everything was, at some point, discovered or created by some enterprising or curious human being. The devices you use daily, the symbols making up the language you're reading right now, the mechanics of the electricity powering your home, all the medical marvels that went into keeping you alive and well in this moment... (Ignore the fact that someone once had to look at a cow and decide "I will try to drink whatever comes out of these pink things.")

Each of these accomplishments had to be fought for and won, one tiny step at a time. Much of what our modern world is made of comes directly from the diligent effort of people working to understand the universe—and create their own inventions. All this scientific and technological progress was made not simply by sheer force of will or strength, but by using the scientific method, and seeing the world in a way that prioritizes rational argument founded on sound empirical or logical data. In other words, *the experiment* is a mental tool so immense, so valuable, and so central to the survival of our species that it's hard to imagine where we'd be without it. It takes us from point A to point B, and it lets us know that we are directly affecting the world we inhabit.

Instead of cowering in the face of the unknown, the experiment allows you to systematically and logically ask questions of the world around you, and make sense of the answers. It's a tool to gradually pull back ignorance and reveal useful facts and information, unearth new possibilities, or show us where we've made an error.

Of course, in this classical view, you may be thinking of the quintessential "experiment": a scientist in a lab poking around with test tubes or wires, or a clinical trial for a new medication. The truth is, we conduct experiments all the time, formally and informally, consciously and unconsciously. Any time we deliberately manipulate conditions around us and carefully note the outcome, we are doing an experiment. Granted, not every experiment is going to be rigorous or perfectly sound! Nevertheless, experimentation is a method of patterning and understanding our encounters with the world. The concept behind this book is that some of the best experiments *can be done with nothing more than your mind.*

Eons ago, humans had to learn things the hard way: if you wanted to know if a berry was poisonous or not, you ate it and hoped for the best. But, if you survived, everyone could learn from your actions without having to incur any risk themselves. Gradually, people could build on what they already knew so that less and less had to be done concretely, out there in the world. This is somewhat less efficient, and such experiments cannot always be seen.

Thought experiments are conducted in a similar spirit. If we explore new ideas, arguments and scenarios *mentally* rather than literally, we're freed from so many limitations. What would be impossible or impractical to do physically is possible with nothing more than careful thought.

Thought experiments are not subject to any moral or natural laws, can be done relatively quickly and have (for the most part!) no real-world consequences. Their strength is that they give us the opportunity to fully flesh out certain hypothetical possibilities without committing to them practically. They allow us to discover aspects of ourselves we might not have otherwise, and think of the ramifications of certain possible acts long before we are technologically capable of them. There are countless innovators who, if asked where their inspiration came from, will point to speculative sci-fi from centuries prior, or whimsical "what if" questions that spurred their curiosity.

The thought experiments we'll be exploring in this book have all served a particular purpose in their historical context. However, in learning about them, we teach ourselves to reach outside our own habitual thoughts and beliefs. What philosophy in general, and thought experiments in particular, can teach us is twofold: firstly, that we are inhabiting a *way* of thinking at all, and secondly, that our way of thinking can be changed.

As you read on, the hope is that you'll develop your own critical thinking skills, mental agility and self-awareness. You'll get comfortable *thinking about thinking*— perhaps the most valuable and transferable skill there is! By learning to carefully consider the virtues and drawbacks of the very process of thinking itself, you give yourself the opportunity to spot bias, question assumptions, more deeply understand your beliefs and—if you're lucky—open the door to a completely new idea.

Thought experiments are like a grand arena where you can take your brain out to play, to explore and to learn about itself, to grow larger and more robust. The ability to see not just *what is* but also *what could be* is fundamental to any endeavor that requires creativity or problem-solving acumen. It also helps you shift perspectives if necessary and consider something we seldom do: that we might be wrong! Manipulating thoughts, information, multiple variables, and coming up with an answer (for which there is no true right or wrong—a learned ability in itself) is something that can be applied to every walk of life.

Throughout history, thought experiments have allowed great thinkers and philosophers to see beyond their immediate grasp, to ask far-ranging questions and push the limits of human knowledge. Using thought experiments in your own life, however, will make you a more focused, more robust thinker with a cognitive and intellectual scope far wider than if you'd never challenged yourself in this particular way.

Finally, perhaps the most important benefit to engaging in thought experiments is that you give yourself the chance to chew over questions for which there simply *isn't* an answer, even with infinitely advanced scientific, technological or philosophical tools. Training your brain to confidently engage with these sorts of questions is enriching beyond the quick satisfaction of solving a problem or optimizing what you already know.

So, let's look a little closer: what exactly constitutes a thought experiment? Is it merely a question, simply asking "what if?"

Well, yes and no. The spark of wonder and curiosity is certainly the beginning, but a well-conducted thought experiment is also about the careful analysis of your answer, of other peoples' answers, and how to interpret them.

A big part of a thought experiment is thoroughly considering the consequences and implications of certain conditions, actions or choices. It's more along the lines of, "What happens IF such-and-such is true?" Thought experiments are completely fabricated "conditionals"—they are fictions which can obliquely bring us around to truths, or at the least illuminate our limitations, assumptions or errors. A truly great thought experiment often spurs further questions—a sign that your mind is mentally exploring an entirely new theoretical space. You may get surprising answers to questions and the opportunity to completely change your worldview—without the bother of having to actually *do* anything!

Thought experiments require us to apply our imagination, to entertain hypotheticals, and follow through potential outcomes and ramifications without actually trying them out for "real." When people encounter new scientific, political or cultural developments, they extrapolate and may start to think about possible future worlds—what would it look like if the DNA for every plant was owned by a corporation? If we take some commonly held tenets and follow them to their full conclusion, where do we land?

In our mind's eye, we see our best guess of the outcome, or a predicted conclusion, modeled on what we know now. We take our time to contemplate circumstances that aren't the case, can never be the case, or which we don't wish to be the case. Essentially, a thought experiment allows us to carry out "tests," but in the laboratory of our minds.

The Problem of the Runaway Trolley

Consider a seemingly simple hypothetical situation: you are standing and watching a train that's headed right for five people tied to the tracks, who will certainly be killed if the train continues. If you pull a lever, the train will divert and head down another track, killing instead just a single person tied to that track. So, if you fail to act, five people die, but if you do act, only one person dies. The question is, would you pull the lever? Why?

Now, the idea is not to say, "That would never happen, so who cares?" The situation, obviously, is contrived. But it forces us to think outside the box and take a closer look at our default mental models. It invites us to have a conversation beyond what is immediately and concretely in front of us.

Simply by asking the question, you have participated in one of philosophy's classic thought experiments, the so-called Trolley Problem. You may be spurred to think all kinds of new thoughts, strengthening different modes of reasoning just as an athlete trains different muscles of their body:

You may wonder, if we think a single life is important, does it imply that five lives are five times as important? Here you're grappling with utilitarianism. You may believe most people would act to minimize harm if given the chance, considering what you know of how people normally behave (deductive reasoning), or you may wonder if not acting in this case completely absolves a person of guilt (now you're thinking about moral philosophy).

You may wonder, what if the single person was your child or parent? What if you had to physically push a person in front of the train to stop it? What if each of the five people had cancer and was going to die within the next year? What if there were five babies, yet the lone person standing was akin to Albert Einstein or some other genius? What if you had the power to sacrifice yourself in their places? What plea would you make if you were the single person? Now you're practicing switching perspectives and views.

If you ask yourself whether saving a family member versus a stranger is any more ethical, you're actively seeking and evaluating support for this argument. You might think the whole situation over and decide that it's implicitly OK to do wrong if it prevents a larger wrong from occurring. Congratulations—you've made a hypothesis. You could "test" this hypothesis (not an opinion) by asking whether pulling the lever should result in being punished by the law. You could make a prediction about what would happen if this was actually the case, in the real world, and on and on...

As you can see, one hypothetical situation can stimulate a whole new world of critical thinking, in every direction.

In fact, people have been chewing over the trolley problem for years, teasing apart what it can tell us about how we think about culpability, the value of human life, moral behavior and psychology, the limits of a utilitarian approach in philosophy, and more. Many variants have been dreamt up too—for example, what if the single person was a villain?

While such thought experiments might seem glib—and perhaps a little unsettling— they do serve a useful purpose. They are used by philosophers to investigate what beliefs we hold to be true and, as a result, what kind of knowledge we can have about ourselves and the world around us. Sometimes, that process will be a little bizarre or unpleasant. But sometimes, it can also push us beyond our limits and open up new and different perspectives.

Long story short, thought experiments teach us to think.

In the chapters that follow, we'll delve into famous thought experiments that have been carried out throughout history, and their surprising ramifications. We'll look at ancient and modern philosophers alike, as well as physicists and great thinkers from all over the world. Many classical thought experiments have had profound effects on the way we think about ourselves in the modern world, so at the very least, learning about what each one implies will give you a richer insight into mankind's philosophical development through the ages.

The Zombie Cat

Let's begin with the famous but often-misunderstood thought experiment of *Schrodinger's cat*. To understand the point that physicist Erwin Schrodinger was trying to make, we need to know a little about the state of theoretical physics at the time, including the Copenhagen Interpretation. Niels Bohr and Werner Heisenberg were proponents of this interpretation of quantum mechanics in the 1920s, and used it to explain and conceptualize some strange results found in quantum mechanics experiments. Under this interpretation, physical systems demonstrate what's called "wave function collapse," which simply means that their properties are only definite once measured—and quantum mechanics can only show us the *probabilities* of a certain outcome. Importantly, the Copenhagen Interpretation is only one of many interpretations of quantum theory, each with their own support and criticisms, of which Schrodinger's cat is also only one.

The thought experiment goes like this: imagine there is a cat placed inside a box for an hour. Inside the box is a Geiger counter (which can measure radioactive particles), a small container of radioactive material, a hammer and a little vial of cyanide that will kill the cat if broken.

The radioactive material is set up in such a way as to allow for a 50 percent *chance* that after the hour has passed, a single atom of the material will decay (it's not important to understand radioactive decay, only that radioactive elements are unstable and liable to emit particles, i.e. radioactivity). The setup is such that if a particle is emitted, the Geiger counter records it and the hammer drops, breaking the vial and killing the cat.

Schrodinger argued that, using the Copenhagen Interpretation, you could say that the cat *is literally both dead and alive* before you open the box to confirm the case. In other words, it exists in some strange state where it is simultaneously living and deceased, and only opening the box collapses the uncertainty.

If this sounds kind of weird to you, that's the point. Schrodinger used this thought experiment to highlight how uncertainty at the subatomic level could have strange implications for bigger objects—like cats. This thought experiment forms just a small part of a large and complex conversation in theoretical physics, and is beyond the scope of this book. However, even without understanding the details, one can see why the experiment has been so useful.

In this branch of physics, measurement of phenomena itself was under question—so normal experimentation was out of the question. When trying to understand things like probability distributions, whether light is a particle or a wave, what constitutes measurement and so on, we *have to* resort to thought experiments.

Schrodinger thus used a purely hypothetical situation in lieu of a real-world experiment to make his point. He took a premise from an accepted model and asked, "What happens if we think this way for large objects?" This scenario, like the Trolley Problem, has inspired many subsequent thought experiments. Indeed, much of theoretical physics plays out in this abstract, purely mathematical space, far outside the lab.

What can this thought experiment teach the layperson about critical thinking? Often, the flaws in our arguments or beliefs can be found if we merely follow our own models to their full conclusion. In other words, we use thought experiments to fully consider all the implications of our perspective—i.e., if such-and-such is the case, what does it mean for everything else? In Schrodinger's case, the sheer implausibility of the outcome was an implied criticism. In considering any argument or point of view, ask yourself: How would the world have to be if my theory were true? *Is* the world that way? What does my argument imply? Are the implications desirable/logical/true? And if not, does it invalidate my original argument?

This might appear to epitomize one of the loudest criticisms of philosophy, that it is a bunch of circuitous thinking with no real ending or purpose. However, this endless analysis and prodding of your thoughts is the real purpose in enriching yourself.

Physics First

Before we delve completely into thought experiments that are more about how we think and how we can finetune our thinking abilities, let's take a brief look at two other instances in which thought experiments helped advance science in very real ways.

Thought experiments were one of Einstein's superpowers. He could imagine a scenario, play it out mentally with shocking accuracy and detail, and then extract the subtle conclusions that lay within.

One of Einstein's most famous *Gedankenexperiments* (literally German for "thought experiment") begins with a simple premise: What would happen if you chased and then eventually caught up to and rode a beam of light through space? In theory, once you caught up to the beam of light, it would appear to be frozen next to you because you are moving at the same speed. Just like if you are walking at the same pace as a car driving next to you, there is no acceleration (the relative velocities are the same), so the car would seem to be stuck to your side.

The only problem was that this was an impossible proposition at the turn of the century. If you catch up to the light and the light appears to be frozen right next to you, then it is inherently impossible that it is light, because of the difference in speeds. It ceases to be light at that moment. This means one of the rules of physics was broken or disproved with this elementary thought.

Therefore, one of the assumptions that underlay physics at the time had to change, and Einstein realized that the assumption of time as a constant needed to shift. This discovery directly laid the path for the theory of relativity. The closer you get to the speed the light, the more time becomes different for you—relative to an outside observer.

This thought experiment allowed Einstein to challenge what were thought to be set-in-stone rules set forth by Isaac Newton's three laws of energy and matter. This thought experiment was instrumental in realizing that people should have questioned old models and fundamental "rules" instead of trying to conform their theories to them.

Before Einstein came Isaac Newton, of course known for discovering the concept of gravity and putting forth the three laws of motion. A corollary to these tenets was thinking through the specifics of how gravity could create something like a standard planetary orbit. This is generally known as Newton's Cannon, and it proceeds like this:

Suppose you fire a cannon horizontally from a high mountain. The cannonball will obviously fall to earth at some point, because of the pull of the earth's gravitational forces, directly toward the center of the earth. As you shoot the cannonball with more force and velocity, it will of course travel further and further before being dragged back down to earth by gravity.

What if the cannonball was fired with the exact right amount of velocity and force, such that it would travel completely around the earth and be perpetually falling, as it was still caught in earth's gravitational pull, but never quite falling before it reached the earth's horizon? This is an orbit! And this is how Newton, hundreds of years ago, deduced that the orbit of the earth's moon functioned: it continuously fell in its path around the earth. (He was right!)

Practical applications aside, we'll now begin to explore the depths of our thinking.

Takeaways:

- A thought experiment is much more than a "what if" scenario played out to its logical or philosophical end. It's a grand arena where you can take your brain out to learn, explore, grow, and play. It's how you can truly learn to think and conceive of the world outside of your own perspective. Some thought experiments will force you to expand your mind in certain ways, while others will encourage you to utilize novel perspectives and lines of thought. Using thought experiments in your own life will make you a more focused, more robust thinker with a cognitive and intellectual scope far wider than if you'd never challenged yourself in this particular way. Learn to search for an answer, even when there is no true correct or wrong way of thinking. Stretch your thinking capabilities and boundaries and see how things look afterwards.

- A prime example of mulling around solutions and perspectives for which a million variables exist is the Trolley Problem. Would you rather allow one person to die or five? This is a classic thought experiment that forces you into a series of escalating moral dilemmas. It makes you consider who you are, and what you value, and why that is. In the end, nothing is solved or clarified, except your own thoughts. There is no answer except to systematically learn and explore.

- More practical applications of thought experiments come in the form of Schrodinger's cat (molecular structure), Albert Einstein's riding a wave (relativity and the speed of light), and Newton's Cannon (gravity and orbits). These theories mostly concerned hard sciences, and explored them in a way that was impossible at the time (and still is currently). Today, we might have computers to map out simulations and projections, but thought experiments are still able to touch the unknown and the unquantifiable.

- Get comfortable thinking about thinking, because that's what we'll be doing throughout the book. The thought experiments we'll be exploring in this book have all served a particular purpose in their historical context. However, in learning about them, we achieve the broader goal of teaching ourselves to reach outside our own habitual thoughts and beliefs.

Chapter 2. The Nature of Uncertainty

Thought alone can take us to new and surprising places. We've seen with Schrodinger's cat that thought experiments allow us to grapple with phenomena in the natural world that simply *can't* be measured in the ordinary ways. Let's now turn to how thought experiments can be used to help us tackle ideas from an entirely different realm of knowledge. What can thought experiments teach us about the nature of reality itself, as well as our ability to access and understand it?

The early philosophers didn't take long to paint themselves into a corner. As they used their powers of logic and reasoning to fashion a picture of the world and their place in it, they inevitably came to ask: what about our thought itself? What are the differences between what we *think* we know and what we do actually know—and how could we ever measure the distance between the two?

Shadows Vs. Reality

The next thought experiment is again a fictitious, allegorical situation designed to draw attention to the nature of our perception, the ways we can be ignorant and not know it, what it means to be educated, and our own intrinsic capacity for expanding our conscious awareness. The thought experiment is Plato's "*allegory of the cave*" and is essentially concerned with the branch of philosophy called *epistemology*. Very simply, this branch includes those theories and models concerning knowledge of reality itself. What *is* knowledge (or beliefs, theories, ideas, even truth), can humans be said to have knowledge, and if so, how?

A very simple thought experiment will quickly show you how far-reaching these questions can be: Right now, try to think of something you know. Now, ask yourself, how do you know it? If you "know" that the sky is blue, well, have you literally checked today? Or are you simply expecting it to be blue because it was yesterday when you looked? And if you looked, are you really sure it is in fact blue, and not some other color, like white? What does it even mean for something to be blue anyway, and if both you and your friend believe you've seen blue, how could you ever be sure that you were both alluding to the *same* set of neural impulses in your respective visual cortices? Really, do you "know" the sky is blue just because you've been told it is? It might interest you to know that certain cultures have wildly different color-naming conventions (the Russians have two distinct words for two distinct colors that Americans simply call blue), and the Candushi tribe in Peru don't even bother having words for colors.

These questions may seem a little circular or redundant, but in asking them we're warming up our brains to tackle others like them. What's the best way to think about the things you can't think about? Consider the world you live in and you're sure to see how valuable a skill this is! Mental flexibility, critical thinking, the ability to reflexively *see yourself think* and adjust given incomplete information—these are the things that make a person intelligent.

On to Plato's cave allegory. The setup is as follows. Imagine a dark cave where some prisoners are held captive for their entire lives, and cannot turn their heads around to look behind them. They are chained so as to look straight ahead to the cave wall in front of them. Behind them is a fire. Between the prisoners and the fire is a pathway, along which people can walk—"puppeteers"— and the things they carry will naturally cast a shadow on the wall in front of the prisoners.

So, the prisoners never see the real items passing behind them; they only see the elaborate shadows cast on the wall. Perhaps they also hear echoes of whatever is passing by. Plato then asks, what would the experience and reality of these prisoners be? He said they would take the shadows for reality itself, thinking them real and not just reflections of the real. They would not understand the *cause* of the shadows, they would merely see the end result and mistakenly believe it to be reality.

An object would pass behind them and cast a shadow—maybe a book, in the allegory (a symbol for learning and wisdom)—and the prisoners would say "I see a book." However, we, knowing better, would know that the prisoner is wrong—he sees a *shadow* of a book, but doesn't know it. Plato then asks us, What is the nature of the claim this prisoner makes? When he uses the word "book," what is he actually talking about?

Plato says that, not knowing any better, the prisoners would completely believe that the word "book" referred to the particular shadow they saw on the walls. Without being able to turn around, they would never know what a "real" book is. They'd use their language as we all do—to point to things in their experience. Importantly, they would not feel as though they were wrong. They would have no idea that they were mistaken. In fact, it would be akin to esteemed scientists of days gone by who claimed resolutely that the earth was the center of the universe, or that the body was ruled over by four humors. The claim "I see a book" is exactly like their claim, "I have knowledge. I *know* this."

Now, as we've seen before, thought experiments are typically used to make some point the author wants to emphasize in a particular context. In this case, Plato had a theory of "Forms" he wished to draw attention to with this allegory. Though this classical view of Forms is only of historical interest today, Plato hoped the allegory would help people better grasp his unusual ideas. To him, language doesn't refer to the literal things in front of us, but to Forms, i.e., abstractions that are physically incarnated in the real world but exist primarily in the mind.

In other words, there can exist a form called "blue" on its own, independent of any material manifestation. For Plato, being ignorant of the world of Forms was like being the prisoner who didn't know about real objects except for the shadows they cast. In Plato's conception, the things we see around us are mere shadows of the unseen, abstract Forms. We don't need to follow along with this particular argument to derive value from Plato's allegory.

For Plato, being able to turn your head and educate yourself on the real sources of your immediate experience is akin to learning about his Forms. (He was, ironically and unfortunately, rather wedded to his ideas and took pity on those who didn't agree with him!) Though there are many problems with Plato's conception, the cave allegory is nevertheless a useful exercise. It shines a light on the way we use language, how we pattern our experience and the consequences it might have for ever grasping the "real world"—if that's possible.

It's a simple yet powerful thought: *what we see* might not be the same as *what is*, and in fact what we see has as much to do with what's in front of us as our own nature as observers. Plato believed fervently that education and intellectual refinement were humankind's highest virtue and redeemer. But it all begins with the ability to recognize your own potential ignorance—via doubt.

How many of us go about life as though there was nothing in our world that we didn't fully grasp? When was the last time you truly considered your alternatives, or any potential gaps or errors in your thinking? It can be one of the most difficult but also most illuminating exercises: What if you're wrong, or only seeing a tiny part of the truth? What if your ideal solution is invisible to you right now?

Plato likened a philosopher to a prisoner who has managed to escape, and who perhaps has the task of trying to explain what he's seen. He believed the ordinary public to be ignorant and resistant to education. The allegory also draws neat lines between two modes of gaining knowledge: direct experience through the senses, or via reason and argument that is independent of the senses.

Like the prisoners, we only know the world through the narrow aperture of our own limited sensory experience. If we were to figuratively rise from our imprisonment and see the world from a higher realm, would we even comprehend it? Thought experiments that ask us to imagine life in six dimensions or worlds where time doesn't exist can perhaps give us a sense of what Plato was getting at.

There are many questions that come from Plato's allegory. What is truly accessible through human senses and intellect? Is it even possible to go beyond those limits? Is there a world outside of our experience of it, neutral and abstract, and is it possible to access it beyond our ordinary perceptions? In a way, each of us is in our own private cave, unable even to accurately confirm that our neighbor is using the same rules for assigning words to shadows. The glaring of the sun on eyes that have never seen it before could be damaging—a prisoner returning from the outside world would not be able to communicate what he'd seen, and would be temporarily blinded. Would the other prisoners even *want* to follow his lead?

Without getting embroiled in the finer details of Plato's philosophy (of which there are many), we can see the spirit of the enquiry: the big deal here is that, like the prisoners, we too could be laboring under a falsehood and never know it. Right now, at this moment, what are you ignorant of?

By design, an impossible question to answer!

When was the last time you even entertained the possibility that what you think is completely, utterly wrong? It might be anyone's guess just how much we can educate ourselves and expand our minds, but one thing is true: none of it is possible unless we are willing to first acknowledge the *possibility* of being wrong. Nobody walks around consciously making room for the fact that they may be operating in ignorance. But what if we did?

The first step—perhaps the biggest step—is to really internalize the idea that our perceptions of things and the things themselves are not necessarily identical. The objects that created our sense perceptions are distinct from the perceptions themselves. It's easy to get comfy inside our own sense-caves, but we can always peek out periodically. Even if we can't literally turn our heads and take in reality "for real," we can use our minds, logic, and rational thought to help us get a little closer.

How can this thought experiment improve the quality of our own thinking?

Plato's experiment connects closely with the age-old maxim that *the map is not the territory.*" We can use maps (ideas and symbols) to helps us navigate reality, but the correspondence is never perfect, and we should be careful not to forget that we have made an analogy at all—our conceptions of reality are not identical with reality.

Maps are, necessarily, simplified abstractions that omit plenty of key information. They are like models of the world, mere sketched outlines to help us better understand reality. If you forget that you are using a map at all, you may overlook these inherent limitations and weaknesses, and be tripped up by them as a result. The map is always going to be a best guess, a snapshot, a simplification. These maps need to evolve, and this isn't possible if you are never truly cognizant of the fact that you are using one in the first place.

Consider a simple example, one popularized by Nassim Taleb, author of *The Black Swan*. One may spend ages with the idea or model that "swans are white" and never have occasion to question this. However, some swans are occasionally black. Discovering one would force you to update your mental model after the fact. It's fine to be surprised by a black swan, and no big deal to change your model to "swans are usually white, but can be black sometimes."

But what if the thing you don't know is more important than the color of a swan? The real trouble comes when unexpected events are bigger and more impactful—like a financial crash. How can we become better at predicting the unpredictable, or, more fundamentally, knowing what we don't know? For Taleb, the issue is that humans rely too much on what they already "know," and don't actively seek out what they lack knowledge of. In other words, they hold tightly to the maps they have and are caught off guard when they discover inaccuracies, or completely new territories they're unprepared to navigate. We get too comfortable with the models we have in the moment, and fail to take risks, seize opportunities or reward new ideas; we're like the prisoners in the cave who take the shadows in front of them as reality, and don't ask any further questions.

So, in the real world, economists, financiers, market forecasters, trend analysts, business gurus and all manner of social or cultural prophets make claims on what the future holds, forgetting that the data they're using is incomplete, and that they have not factored into their model the very likely possibility of being blindsided by an unpredictable or unforeseen event. We *need* models, yet these models always *will* have limitations. In a way, asking what our tools can't do makes them more effective than merely assuming they can do it all, and then being proven wrong when we attempt to use them to solve problems they can't solve.

We always narrow down our focus to make our appraisals of life simpler and more manageable. We look at just a few facts, or just one location, only a handful of people, or consider only a few factors or features. But it's essential to zoom out again. We must not allow ourselves to believe that these mental shortcuts are in any way the same as reality itself.

Thinking like a philosopher allows you to temporarily glimpse behind you, rather than getting engrossed in the endless shadows playing in front of you. It's habitually asking "in what ways could I be wrong?" instead of "where can I find evidence that I'm right?" It's this willingness to look at things one or two layers deeper that characterizes a higher quality of thought. While most people, most of the time work on the superficial level—the level of habit, assumption, unexamined sensation and knee-jerk perception—it is possible to look beyond.

Inside the Matrix

A related philosophical thought experiment gets to the heart of some very big questions in a similar way. It's called the *"brain in a vat."* Even if you've never heard of it before, if you've watched the classic sci-fi film *The Matrix*, you're already familiar with its premise.

If you read a little philosophy and pay attention to what is happening in the world of AI, you can't help but ask eventually, "What if *my life* is just one big computer simulation?" Like the poor hapless people imprisoned unwittingly in the machine called the Matrix, you could, at this very moment, be living out an elaborate fantasy world while the "real you" is elsewhere—or perhaps doesn't exist at all. Perhaps a genius mastermind has merely constructed a very convincing facsimile of the real world and trapped you inside it. This is philosopher Hilary Putman's classic thought experiment legacy, but it was in turn inspired by Descartes and his ideas in his 1637 *"Discourse on the Method of Rightly*

Conducting One's Reason and of Seeking Truth in the Sciences."

But before we examine this idea, we must address the question of how you know you're, say, sitting on your living room sofa and reading. Your sense organs tell you. But then, what if this genius mastermind (or a deceiving demon) at some point removed your brain from your body and placed it in a vat of nutrients in a lab, with every nerve connected to a computer? You'd be fed all the data necessary to give your sense perception the belief that it was inside the living room, reading.

Here come the obvious questions: Are you even alive? Are you still *you*? Would the world you live in still count as real? Would you care? And the biggest question of all: how do you know that this isn't the case already, right now? We are back in Plato's cave again, and don't know what we don't know.

Descartes thought about this kind of a thing a lot, and the best he could come up with was the attitude that absolute ignorance was a great starting point; then one could carefully build up only what one *100 percent knew* to be true. Let's begin, as Descartes would suggest, by doubting all things. Now, what can be trusted? Let's consider the sense perceptions. Can you trust that the book or device you're holding right now is really there? Maybe, but then again, senses can be wrong sometimes, for example if you're ill, insane, or deceived by a demon. So, let's forget about sensory perceptions, and any kind of knowledge built on them (goodbye scientific method!).

What else do we know? Can we determine, with absolute certainty, that we ourselves exist, then? If not, and we say something like, "I possibly don't exist," then there must be someone to have had this thought, someone behind the "I" in the sentence. So, even if in doubt, we can know that we ourselves exist. So far so good. Here we have the basis of Descartes' famous "I think, therefore I am."

Following down this path, Descartes assures us that even if we were a brain in a vat—or indeed at the mercy of an evil demon toying with us—we could still say with certainty that we exist. Whether dreaming, living in an illusion, mistaken or ignorant, we can know one thing: there is a "we" to have all these experiences!

If that doesn't seem like much of a triumph, it pays to remember again that thought experiments can always be updated and used for our own ends, in our modern world. Considering this experiment in terms of the nature of reality and uncertainty, we can see that it teaches us something quite uncommon: the dedication to take nothing, absolutely *nothing* for granted. It may seem a little extreme, but occasionally looking at the world completely stripped of every working model, every assumption you have, can reveal a depth of clarity that will only enhance your thinking.

This thought experiment can remind us of the power of getting right down to basics again. Brilliant detectives often do this kind of work naturally. A detective may look at a random assortment of facts in front of him and have to reconstruct past events to understand what happened, who's culpable and, more importantly, whether it can be proven in court "beyond a reasonable doubt." Legal and judicial minds practice this kind of thinking often, but we can benefit too. Wipe the slate clean and ask, what do I *really* know here?

Perhaps a situation looks like a robbery. But do I *know* that yet? I can choose to suspend my decision until I have further evidence. Have I actively considered other scenarios that might present themselves to look exactly like a robbery without actually being one? Or am I merely looking for evidence for a conclusion I've already unconsciously reached? Good detectives are often not those who can spin fantastical scenarios from shreds of info and clues (like Sherlock Holmes), but rather hard-nosed sceptics in the philosophical sense.

You can do the same in your own life. CBT, or cognitive behavioral therapy, is a little like having a mini skeptic on your shoulder. If you suffer from anxiety, you may tell yourself, "That guy recognized me and didn't wave hello. I bet he hates me." Use the lessons from the brain-in-a-vat experiment to test these assumptions.

Can you really know that he hates you? Could your sense perceptions (or indeed your anxiety) be fooling you right now? Can you find evidence that a person who doesn't hate you could still act in that way? (Yes, you can—you did the same thing last week to someone you genuinely like). So, have you stumbled upon an unshakeable law of the universe or is it merely a thought your brain has come up with, bearing little resemblance to reality?

Blame it on our human ego needing to feel certain and not enjoying the state of ignorance, but we often tend to avoid starting from zero, and will sometimes begin with any old assumption if it only means we don't have to start with nothing.

But starting from nothing forces you to have a curious "beginner's mindset" and gives you the gift of seeing a situation as neutrally as possible. Doubting everything puts a big spotlight on all your assumptions and asks whether they're really pulling their weight or not. It can feel like such a loss to admit that much of what you take as a given is not necessarily true; but then again, if your beliefs weren't true, you were better off acknowledging the fact than carrying on with illusions or misunderstandings.

Finding "the truth" is not easy, but it's far easier when you aren't carrying around the baggage of all the things you wish were true. Do you remember when Neo first leaves the Matrix, and Morpheus welcomes him into the completely empty "desert of the real"? Leaving a world of illusion is always a little scary but at some point, we all have to choose between the red or blue pill!

Thinking this way might mean that, when asked what you can truly know, you come up with "nothing," but then at least you are functioning clearly: we all take risks, make assumptions and use incomplete models. It's best to know, at the very least, that this is in fact what you are doing. Your understanding may be nothing more than realizing that you don't know what you thought you did—but how monumental a leap that really is!

A Loss of Control

Recall that Descartes' general method of doubt involved searching for firsthand evidence and proof, and trying to inject a bit of certainty into knowledge by starting from ground zero. This was a roundabout way to say that our reasoning abilities cannot always be trusted—a self-evident truth as we are always subject to cognitive biases, skewed perspectives, and simple errors. This is what is typically referred to as Descartes' *demon* problem.

> I shall then suppose, not that God who is supremely good and the fountain of truth, but some evil genius not less powerful than deceitful, has employed his whole energies in deceiving me; I shall consider that the heavens, the earth, colours, figures, sound, and all other external things are nought but the illusions and dreams of which this genius has availed himself in order to

lay traps for my credulity; I shall consider myself as having no hands, no eyes, no flesh, no blood, nor any senses, yet falsely believing myself to possess all these things; I shall remain obstinately attached to this idea, and if by this means it is not in my power to arrive at the knowledge of any truth, I may at least do what is in my power and with firm purpose avoid giving credence to any false thing, or being imposed upon by this arch deceiver, however powerful and deceptive he may be.

Translation? We can't be sure that our reasoning abilities are trustworthy, honest, reliable, or correct. Descartes puts forth an argument to prove his point, just like before. If we think about a simple addition problem such as 2+3=5, then there are two possibilities about how we reach the answer. The first possibility is that our powers of reasoning are indeed reliable and sound, and thus we are calculating correctly.

The second possibility is that an evil demon from the depths of the earth is manipulating our brain, and we only come to the conclusion that 2+3=5 because the demon puts that idea in our minds. Here, we come to an answer via deception and a profound lack of correct reasoning.

Thus, we can only trust our sense of reasoning if we can ensure that the second possibility, and ones like it, never occurs. But that's not possible. We can't ensure that our sense of reasoning is reliable or absolute truth—not by itself, anyway. Thus, we can only rely on firsthand evidence or experiences.

This can be a highly disconcerting notion— to not be able to trust your own reasoning and thought processes. If you can't trust your senses or thoughts, then in what sense is your view of the world real or accurate? What, if anything, can provide the type of certainty that Descartes so desires? That is the very conundrum Descartes dealt with and strove to overcome.

On a final note concerning uncertainty, lack of knowledge, and the inevitable level of ignorance we are burdened with, let's take a look into Taoist philosophy. One of the most famous parables, or thought experiments, comes from the Chinese philosopher Zhuangzi, who is generally considered the second-most important figure after Lao-Tzu in Taoism. He asserted that one day he fell asleep and dreamed that he was a butterfly.

> *Once upon a time, I, Zhuangzi, dreamt I was a butterfly, fluttering hither and thither, to all intents and purposes a butterfly. I was conscious only of my happiness as a butterfly, unaware that I was Zhuangzi. Soon I awakened, and there I was, veritably myself again. Now I do not know whether I was then a man dreaming I was a butterfly, or whether I am now a butterfly, dreaming I am a man. Between a man and a butterfly there is necessarily a distinction. The transition is called the transformation of material things.*

When he woke up, Zhuangzi did not know whether he really was a man who had dreamed he was a butterfly, or whether he was a butterfly now dreaming he was a man. Was it such a realistic dream that he couldn't tell the difference? How would he ever know? How can any of us ever know?

What we believe simply may not be true. In fact, our senses and reasoning may be deceiving us. What we feel so incredibly certain of (being a human and not a butterfly)—well, think twice.

Takeaways:

- Uncertainty is a very uncomfortable concept to wrap our minds around. The human brain highly prefers a concrete answer, thought, or even guess. It's why we jump to conclusions and prioritize speed over accuracy. Learning to thrive in the limbo of uncertainty can greatly benefit your thinking skills because it teaches you to slow down, check your assumptions, put away your ego, and embrace the ultimate version of "I have no idea." Once you can accept this starting point, the world will suddenly open up—because you are listening and observing.

- We kick the chapter off with a thought experiment dubbed Plato's Cave. It tells the tale of prisoners shackled in a dark cave facing inside, so the only thing they can see is a series of shadows from people, animals, and events going on outside. Of course, this is not the real world—from our vantage point. But to them, these shadows are everything, and it is unthinkable that anything else exists. So the question comes—how can we ever know if what we are seeing is merely a shadow, or the true form and nature of the thing? Of people? Of ourselves? Accept that perception is necessarily flawed, and attempt to think from the ground up.
- Next, we delve into a thought experiment that you are already familiar with. It's called the brain in a vat experiment, and it closely mirrors (or rather, the other way around) the premise for the movie *The Matrix.* What if we are all indeed just brains in vats of liquid, being externally fed a lifetime of experiences and nutrients? How could we ever know the difference unless we

were physically shown the jar? And then how could we know that this vision was also true and unfiltered and untampered with? We can't. And that's the point. There's more uncertainty, even to our very nature, and we again should cease all assumptions and think and question more thoroughly.

- Next, we have Descartes' demon problem. This can be said to go a step farther, as it assumes that it's possible (a non-zero chance, to be sure) that a demon is possessing you and causing you to reason and analyze incorrectly or unreliably. Thus? We can't trust ourselves. We can only look at evidence and build from there.

- Finally, we come to a short parable and thought experiment that Chinese philosopher Zhuangzi put forth: the butterfly dream. If Zhuangzi dreamt that he was a butterfly, and his dream seemed so genuine as to be reality, who's to say that in his current life as a human, he is not just a butterfly dreaming that he is here? And again, how can we ever be sure, even about our very existence? You already know the answer, and how that should affect your approach to thinking.

Chapter 3. The Nature of the Infinite

The thought experiments we've considered so far have all allowed us, in one way or another, to access certain realms of thoughts that would be impossible by the ordinary methods.

Schrodinger's cat was a way to conduct an "experiment" and observe the results when one of the variables under examination was observation itself. Same with Einstein and Newton's theories. Plato's cave allegory gave us a metaphor to talk about and conceptualize precisely those things we don't know how to talk about—i.e., what we are ignorant of. The Trolley Problem let us analyze where our ethics, morals, and values lie.

Thought experiments can also help us better grasp other unfathomable concepts, like the infinite.

In this chapter, we'll let the magic of thought experiments guide us toward a way to comprehend what might be a truly incomprehensible idea: the idea of the infinitely small, of the infinitely big, of things with no end and no beginning, of forever. You might be tempted to simply shrug your shoulders and wonder what the point of trying to understand the infinite is. But again, this book is not about *solving* any of the paradoxes or puzzles raised by thought experiments. The exercise is not so much in figuring things out, but in using strange and novel problems to sharpen new mental tools that will then be better suited to tackling the smaller problems of everyday life.

In that spirit, what can thinking about the infinite teach us? How can we improve our mental agility and flexibility by "training" it on these seemingly unthinkable thoughts?

Firstly, as with the previous examples, thought experiments aid us in extending our reach and grasp. It's as though we can grab hold of hard-to-conceptualize concepts and bring them more concretely into our everyday world, where we can take a closer look at them. We do this with metaphor, allegory, and what-if scenarios. The thought experiments that follow will all strike you as rather abstract and lofty, but what can you do *practically* with the skills you develop in engaging with these abstractions?

A good thought experiment will shine a light on how we use language, on the assumptions and concepts we take for granted, on our own blind spots. These experiments can also tantalize us, asking us to peek a little further into the unknown, perhaps even inspiring a feeling of deep awe and something bordering on the mystical or poetic—naturally a consequence to be explored in another book!

What do you think of when you hear the word "infinity"? How would you explain this concept to a child, to a creature from another species if they could understand you, or to an alien from another planet?

Human beings have had different answers to this question throughout history. The Aristotelian view was that the universe was finite, and indeed many early civilizations would conceive of the universe as rather limited—it could fit into a cosmic egg or on the back of a turtle, or ended at some fixed point on the horizon or perhaps only extended as far as the furthest visible stars. It may seem obvious to anyone today that there are problems with this view, but the philosopher Lucretius is credited with being the first to actually suggest an argument for why the universe was *not* finite.

The Javelin Tells All

His argument is called "Lucretius' Spear" and is what it sounds like: if, Lucretius argued, the universe is finite (or "bounded"), then what would happen if a man were to go right up to the edge of it all, and throw a javelin past the limit? What would happen? This is not a hypothetical question. If you insist that the universe does in fact have some point at which it ends, then you'd really be stumped to come up with an answer.

If the spear went hurtling onwards, it would mean that you weren't actually at the limit. If the javelin bounced back, well, what was beyond the boundary? If there was something to stop the movement of the javelin, then that means he was not at the edge either.

Lucretius claimed, "For whatever bounds, that thing must itself be bounded likewise; and to this bounding thing there must be a bound again, and so on for ever and ever throughout all immensity." You can see his point. Lucretius hoped, by this thought experiment, to show that the idea of a finite universe simply didn't make sense. He also wanted to illustrate the concept of infinite and how it interacts with so-called boundaries.

Now, take a step back for a moment and survey your own thoughts. What's going on, mentally? Has your mind run off with a potential counterargument? Are you imagining new and creative scenarios inspired by Lucretius' javelin thrower? If so, congratulations; you are already experiencing the benefits of engaging with thought experiments.

The experiment might have indeed convinced you that the universe is infinite and not finite. But there's more. After all, more modern thinking has suggested ways in which the universe can be thought of as both finite and infinite—for given definitions of both.

For example, imagine that all of existence is shaped like a doughnut, the surface of which we move about on. If you traveled on the surface of this doughnut in all directions, you would never technically come to an "edge" or boundary. However, the surface of the doughnut universe is finite in a concrete sense. It's akin to saying that the javelin would race ahead and come flying from behind the javelin thrower, like a person traveling on a Mobius strip would eventually arrive at the same spot they left from.

A thought that might have occurred to you is to try and use the same argument, but for something you have more knowledge of. If someone claimed the *earth* was finite, someone else could make a javelin-style argument: What would happen if you went to the edge of the earth and threw a spear?

Because you already know that "edge of the earth" is in fact nothing more than a misunderstanding, you might be tempted to rethink the concept of "edge of the universe." Here, you are using skillful induction and deduction, groping your way along new concepts, using what is already known to help understand what isn't.

It's likely that Lucretius' early argument, and others like it, gave rise to the more sophisticated topological and mathematical models we have today for conceptualizing the size and scope of the universe. But what we do today with literal spacecraft, probes, mathematical models and theory, we were already attempting long ago with nothing more than our thoughts.

Einstein famously said that one cannot solve a problem at the same level of thinking that created it. In other words, all insight and illumination come from stepping outside of what you feel are the set facts of your world as you see it. This is where science and creativity amount to the same thing: imagination is something that allows you to think what has not been thought of before.

You cannot use the known to construct a truly novel vision—it can only ever serve as a crutch that takes you part of the way. Consider all the major leaps and bounds in mankind's intellectual history, and you'll see that they were all fundamental reimaginings of old rules. Evolution, Freud's unconscious id, relativity... These are not simply improvements on previous models, but compete rethinks of the models themselves, i.e. not progress within a model, but between models, and beyond them.

Without ever having to go "out there" in the world to measure the actual length and breadth of the universe, thought experiments allow us to sharpen our mental tools and make conceptual space to conceive of the answer we are looking for. This may require completely dismantling old ideas by asking questions like: What does it actually mean to say something is "infinite"? Is this a quality that actually exists in the world, or is it more accurately a word that belies our own limited understanding, a linguistic vestige belonging to a level of thinking that posed the "paradox" in the first place?

The juiciest thought experiments have an uncanny way of making us think really hard about the questions we ask. The physicist Heisenberg claimed that, "What we see is not nature itself, but nature exposed to our method of questioning."

You're probably reminded of Schrodinger's cat, but the quote reminds us that the quality of information we have about the world is very much determined by the manner in which we engage with it. Thought experiments are like questions, but in a way they allow us to look back on those questions themselves. What kind of information are we really looking for from the world? How can we get it? What are the best tools to do so, and what's wrong with the ones we currently use?

By turning over Lucretius' experiment in our minds, we invite ourselves to plunge a little deeper. We find ourselves in the company of some of the biggest of big ideas that have occupied man since the dawn of time. Similar arguments have been used to prove (or, curiously enough, disprove) the existence of God—i.e., if there is one meta-being who created everything, then who created the meta-being? What came before the Big Bang, exactly? Or, if you'd like to put a more Eastern spin on the same sort of contemplations, what did your face look like before you were born, and where does the candle flame *go* when you snuff it out?

In thinking about infinity, we are stretching our minds to the furthest reaches. It might not be overstatement to imagine that every question mankind has asked has been inspired in one way or another by this unfathomable mystery all around us.

Perhaps the greatest lesson this kind of mental exercise can teach us is to look beyond even our own conception of the problem, and the assumptions built into our very questions. In the mundane world we are often presented with what look like choices: do you believe in this thing or that thing? Pick a political candidate or opinion or laundry detergent. But what if there is a third option? What if you're mistaken in thinking of it as a choice at all? What if you can choose both, or neither, or what if the entire question is where the problem lies?

Lucretius' thought experiment teaches us to open up a window to other options. Not A or B, but a third variable, something new and as yet unseen. A space where marvelous and unthinkable things can happen. Psychologists , historians and philosophers can busy themselves endlessly with the question of human nature; a monk on the mountain might shrug and ask, who told you there was such a thing as human nature?

Shakespeare, I Presume?

A related but equally mind-boggling train of thought to follow is one you've probably heard of before: the thought experiment concerning an infinite number of monkeys sitting at an infinite number of typewriters, banging the keys randomly. This famous "infinite monkey theorem" helps stretch the bounds of how we think about infinity, but also large numbers and probability.

The theorem goes like this: an infinite number of monkeys, if sat down in front of an infinite number of typewriters for an infinite amount of time, will eventually write, by sheer accident, an exact copy of the complete works of Shakespeare.

In fact, it's more than this—since the monkeys have infinite time, they would in fact produce the complete works of Shakespeare *an infinite number of times over*, along with every other great work, also an infinite number of times. Émile Borel outlined this idea way back in 1913, although we can understand that he used monkeys as a metaphorical stand-in for any random generator of letters.

The mathematical way of putting it is to say that random inputs will produce all possible outputs, given infinite time. The real-world translation is that any problem can be solved, or anything created, if time and resources are infinite.

However, the probability of a monkey actually producing Shakespeare is, although not technically or mathematically zero, very small. For those interested in the maths, there is a theorem proving that the likelihood of monkeys producing Shakespeare under these conditions is exactly 100 percent. However, it might also interest you to know that staff and students from the University of Plymouth conducted a (tongue-in-cheek) real-life experiment, giving a number of monkeys a number of typewriters and watching to see what happened. After a month, unsurprisingly, the monkeys had produced five pages of the letter "S."

Dan Oliver also wrote a computer program that randomly generated letters, and after the equivalent of 42,162,500,000 billion billion monkey-years (stop to think how enormously large that number is), one of the "monkeys" wrote:

VALENTINE. Cease toIdor:eFLP0FRjWK78aXzVOwm)-';8.t

Hilariously, the first nineteen letters of this string can be found in Shakespeare's *Two Gentlemen of Verona*. Other teams with similar programs also produced results from other Shakespeare plays. Computational speed is a natural hard limit to how much can be done practically speaking, but these real-life attempts don't add much to the fundamental question at hand—we will never be in the position to conduct this experiment for real.

So, what can we glean from the monkeys with typewriters theorem? Surely it only has mathematical value? Anything is possible with enough inputs, and conversely, nothing is impossible with enough inputs. You can't rule out anything that has a slight possibility or chance, and you must always account for everything that is possible. Something is possible from almost nothing. It doesn't sound like a revelation, but it's a more eloquent way of encouraging thoroughness and looking at the concept of randomness and serendipity.

As it happens, this "thought experiment" (more properly a proof or theorem) has inspired much debate and criticism. What can we do with the knowledge that although some things are *mathematically* possible, they aren't realistically feasible given what we know about the world (i.e. no resources are infinite, etc.)?

Some thinkers have attempted to use this experiment to show how evolution could have occurred—the analogy is that simple elements, given enough time and resources, will spontaneously assemble themselves into more complex organisms, without the need for an agent to cause it.

A related analogy is designed to show the impossibility of the claim that life did not evolve, but emerged wholly formed. Imagine you were walking on a beach and saw a watch on the sand. How did it get there? The analogy claims that evolutionary theory (or life randomly emerging by itself) is akin to saying the watch elements washed up onto a beach and randomly assembled themselves into a perfectly functioning watch—possible, but enormously unlikely.

The proposed alternative is that a watchmaker made the device—an argument for intelligent design.

Others have commented on the validity of the thought experiment itself. R. G. Collingwood claimed, "Any reader who has nothing to do can amuse himself by calculating how long it would take for the probability to be worth betting on. But the interest of the suggestion lies in the revelation of the mental state of a person who can identify the 'works' of Shakespeare with the series of letters printed on the pages of a book."

His point is that merely producing a string of symbols associated with a work is not the work itself—a classic example of how a thought experiment designed to engage with questions in one realm (random number generation and probability) can be used to inspire questions and dialogue in another (what it means to create art, and the relationship between symbol and its referent).

For many people, complex systems like living organisms are so far removed from abstract mathematical strings of data as to make any metaphor or analogy useless. Some have similarly criticised the analogy as incomplete, saying that for the product to be meaningful you would need to factor in the beliefs, semantic structures, morality, science, linguistic patterns and so on that came from Shakespeare's time—i.e., already banked knowledge that Shakespeare himself would have worked with (and not, as the monkeys would have to, starting from scratch with merely the fifty symbols of a typewriter).

Using this theorem to talk about evolution is tricky for this same reason—selection of the fittest individuals will mean that strings of DNA that "work" will be retained and passed on; it is not as if every organism existing today had to arise from scratch in each instance.

Like most mathematics, the theory doesn't map neatly onto life as we know it. Economists can predict the consumer behavior of "rational" humans only to find their models fail miserably to predict anything. Statistics can be used to make perfectly true claims ("the average person has one breast") that are nevertheless inaccurate, and AI game theory can tell us about actions, choices and solutions that are most optimal, even though to the average human being they make no sense at all (consider the chess-playing AI, Alpha GO, whose style is no longer comprehensible to ordinary human players.)

Borel argued that although some events might seem *mathematically* possible, they are for all intents and purposes impossible. Just because we can *think* about outlandishly huge numbers, it doesn't mean we can easily translate those concepts to our real, flesh-and-blood world.

Of course, there is a *chance* that the sun might rise in the west one day, but it is so unlikely as to be impossible. When we are comfortable understanding what mathematical probabilities actually mean for our lives and the choices we make, we can use thought experiments like this and the insights that come with them to live (and think) better.

Mathematics can allow us to plumb the very outer edges of what is *theoretically* the case, while common sense then enables us to fill in the concrete details using what we see in the real world. Likewise, though we can agree with Descartes in a theoretical sense that we can know nothing, we can still reasonably inhabit the world using our senses and do pretty well.

Though it might not seem like much, this is a monumental shift: knowing the difference between yes and no, luck and probability, chance and circumstances. It tells us the proper place for abstract theory in our lives: it's worth learning the difference between "in theory" and "in practice"!

In Eastern philosophy, great teachers attempt to point to the fundamental limitations of our conception of reality indirectly, by using nonsense stories, jokes, unanswerable questions or statements like, "What is a buddha? Three pounds of flax."

By their nature, these statements are invitations to step outside of the occupied realm of thought and look at life from a wholly different perspective—an elevated one.

Perhaps we can imagine that Western philosophy does the same, only a little more formally. In seemingly bizarre, paradoxical or nonsensical territory, we uncover not the strangeness of reality itself, but our own limits in being able to conceive of it, or represent it in symbols. It is as though the thinking mind, having looked around at the world, gets the idea to turn back and look on itself, and watch itself as it thinks.

What's Half of Half?

The Greek philosopher Zeno's so-called paradoxes have a koan-like quality about them, and do this work of highlighting the very tools we use to engage with the world—specifically how they *are* tools in the first place, and are not perfect.

Zeno's claim: an arrow shot from a bow will never reach its destination. Why? Because first it has to travel halfway. Once it has, it still has to travel half of the remaining distance, and once it has, it still has to travel half of that remaining distance, and so on to infinity.

The arrow will get closer and closer, but never actually arrive. It will pass through an infinite number of halfway points, which (you can see where this is going) will take an infinite amount of time to pass.

There are variations on this theme: Imagine Achilles races with a tortoise, but agrees to give him a hundred-meter head start. By the time Achilles catches up with the tortoise, he finds in the meantime the tortoise has actually moved a further ten meters. He runs to close this gap but finds the tortoise still has a lead, since in the time it took him to run the ten meters the tortoise moved a further one meter. Achilles is the faster runner but will seemingly never catch up to the slower tortoise.

A final variant concerns arrows or moving objects. At any point along an arrow's trajectory, for an infinitely small window of time (i.e. no time) the arrow can be said to be motionless. If the arrow's path is composed of an infinite number of motionless moments, how can it ever move?

When does the arrow ever have time to move? You might have noticed that Zeno's paradoxes predict and predate Heisenberg's uncertainty principle—we cannot measure an object's position and its velocity simultaneously. Perhaps Zeno was so frustrated with this line of thought that he reincarnated as Heinsenberg to finish his work...

So, what shall we make of all this? This is called a paradox because although you could agree with every statement Zeno makes to arrive at this bizarre conclusion, you can plainly see that the conclusion itself is false. Why?

Let's take a closer look at the world that Zeno lived in. As a proponent of the Eleatic school of philosophy, Zeno supposed that physical phenomenon in the world were illusions, and that reality was essentially a single Being that moved perpetually.

When we see something that looks like movement, we are actually only witnessing different perspectives of this one great entity. Zeno's paradox was therefore a way to support this worldview—i.e., "movement" as we understand it is impossible. The paradoxes prove this because we want to say that both the premise and the conclusion are correct, whereas they cannot both be.

Something is fishy, but what? It's easy to disprove the claim "movement is not possible"—simply move. But then what about the argument Zeno makes—what's wrong with it? The problem here may not have anything to do with whether movement is possible or not, or the exercise in halving progressively smaller increments. The problem may be (again) in the translation of abstract concepts into "real world" experience. Perhaps Zeno merely reminded himself and others that the map (i.e., the language and ideas we use to talk about space) is not the territory (reality itself, in its full, unsymbolized nature).

Zeno's paradoxes play out at the interface between maths and life, between concept and reality. Importantly, they may show us how uncomfortable the fit really is: what can seem "intuitively" correct can be shown to be completely wrong mathematically, statistically or theoretically. Could it be that the conception of "infinity" itself is flawed, and so every story based on it will eventually contain strange paradoxes like these?

The ancient Greeks wrestled with similar concepts when they wondered what would happen if you continually cut a thing in half. Physics now tells us that you do not get infinitely smaller and smaller pieces, but at some point, the "rules" change and we can no longer talk of physical particles at all, but probabilistic, phenomenological ones. Perhaps in the same way, Zeno merely invited us to take a closer look at the threshold where one expression of reality borders another.

Physicists have actually tried to solve this problem (like the researchers who literally gave monkeys typewriters) and drew on knowledge of the smallest length possible given the size of electrons, the speed of light and the gravitational constant. They say that there in fact *aren't* infinite lengths to travel along a path—we can calculate multiples of what's called the Planck length. Others have countered: well, if the Planck length is the smallest length possible, you can imagine a triangle with its longest side equal to the Planck length, so then how long are the other sides?

Perhaps you are already getting a sense of what classical philosophers and mathematicians have had to force themselves to accept: that math is not reality. That an expression such as 1/3 is a mathematical, not a physical phenomenon.

What does Zeno teach us about our own thinking? That hypothetical, abstract, theoretically sound conceptions of life are *not the same as life*. In fact, this is a very good argument for not conducting thought experiments at all! We could jokingly say that all of physics is the strange compulsion to break the universe into imaginary chunks, and then the effort of wondering what the rules are that govern the interaction between the chunks, and then assuming you've discovered something mind-blowing when you realize that you are unable to. The problem is not that the chunks (time, space, numbers) are behaving erratically, but in our original error: the claim that there are chunks in the first place.

If you are someone who cares about *literally and actually* improving your real lived experience, at some point you may tire of thought experiments and doubt their applicability. After all, there is and will never be a Trolley Problem set you before you, nobody has yet found an "edge" to existence, and movement clearly occurs. But this is precisely the value of thought experiments: they illuminate, in crystal clarity, the raw value of our mental models, our ideology, our language. They show us the outlines of our thinking—even in places where we didn't think we were thinking, but assumed we were engaging with reality itself in earnest.

What is the proper place of the *word* (the literal pixels or ink on the page, and the shapes of the letters that make up this word in modern-day English) "infinity"? Let's not engage with the concept of infinity, but instead look behind the scenes, at the code or architecture of the word itself—to what phenomena have we assigned this word?

What assumptions have we made in doing so, and are we correct? More than correct— is this label useful? What does it tell us about ourselves, and our universe? If we find an unhappy mix between symbol and referent, does that mean we throw away the symbol, or decide that the referent is wrong somehow? Both? Neither?

There are no answers to these questions, which is universally the case with modern philosophy. But strange verbal and intellectual tangles like these are not just games—they show us important things about how our brains work. Significantly, they give us the option and opportunity to decide if we'd like to continue on in this realm of thought, or think something else.

Takeaways:

- The infinite is one of the most confusing concepts to grasp. The truth is, in reality, things beyond a certain point of frequency or amount (even money) cease to hold any meaning for us. We just can't imagine or visualize them, and thus they become meaningless. And yet, playing with this concept and understanding it a little better will help stretch your thinking and expand your mind. Taking a subject out of the ether and examining it in a reality-based and consequential way can help you extract a few lessons on extremely big, and extremely small, probabilities, and understand why a mathematical construct like 1/3 cannot truly be expressed as a decimal.

- Any discussion of the infinite must begin with the thought experiment of Lucretius' spear. If you contend that the universe if infinite, and then you walk right up to the edge (first of all, what would the edge even constitute), and then you throw a javelin, then what would happen? Would it bounce off something? Would it disappear? Would it just keep sailing because the universe is indeed infinite? What exactly would take place? Thinking through this abstraction makes clear that we have to suspend reality sometimes and redefine what we think is possible. You might even find that you have been asking wrong questions all along by not accounting for what you didn't consider.

- The infinite monkey theorem is just that—what happens when you put an infinite amount of monkeys into a room with typewriters? Well, the law of big numbers and probabilities dictate that eventually, they will produce a word for word script of any of Shakespeare's plays. In truth, this is a nod to how anything is possible with enough inputs, and conversely, nothing is impossible with enough inputs. You can't rule out anything that has a slight possibility or chance, and you must always account for everything that is possible. Something is possible from almost nothing. It doesn't sound like a revelation, but it's a more eloquent way of encouraging thoroughness and looking at the concept of randomness and serendipity.

- Finally, what's half of half? 25 percent. What's half of that? 12.5 percent. What happens when you get to infinitesimal numbers? Do you ever reach zero? Nope. But is that reflective of reality? Nope. That's what Zeno's paradoxes sought to explain: what seems to be apparent and obvious on paper often has no bearing to reality. Once again, the map is not the territory. Zeno's paradoxes play out at the interface between math and life, between concept and reality. Importantly, they may show us how uncomfortable the fit really is: what can seem "intuitively" correct can be shown to be completely wrong mathematically, statistically or theoretically. Could it be that the conception of "infinity" itself is flawed, and so every story based on it will eventually contain strange paradoxes like these?

Chapter 4. The Nature of Existence and Identity

Phew! From questions of what we can know as humans and an attempt to measure infinity, we can move on to an equally lofty topic that has similarly engrossed man for ages: who are we and why are we here?

In this chapter we'll look at those thought experiments that confront the big questions of what constitutes a person, what it means to say that someone is alive and has consciousness, and what our identity is as human beings. What is a thing or person's essence, the one aspect that, if changed, would make them no longer what they are? Are people's identities real, fixed phenomena or are they more like social constructs or artefacts of language (a common outcome for many thought experiments)?

It's one of those questions that seems simple on the surface but can be quite profound when you dig deeper: who are we *really*, and what would it take for us to not be that anymore? Perhaps in answering questions of who and what we are, mankind is indirectly asking what we *are*, and ought to do, i.e. what our purpose and function is in life. In the same way we cast our minds out to take in the full possibilities of time and space, we turn inward and try to understand ourselves and our fellow humans.

Plank by Plank

The thought experiment called "Theseus' ship" is a well-known and poignant place to start off our enquiries. Theseus has a ship. For reasons only he understands, he gradually takes it apart day by day, piece by piece. One day, he removes one wooden board. Is the ship still the same ship after he removes this board? Most people would probably say yes. But if he continues carefully removing pieces, at what point would you say that it *wasn't* the original ship anymore?

Carrying the story further, imagine that instead of simply removing pieces from the ship, Theseus removed parts and then replaced them with different parts. Is the ship still the same ship, or something different? If so, at what point exactly does it become a different ship? Finally, imagine that instead of just removing parts, Theseus took the individual pieces and reassembled them elsewhere. Where is Theseus' original ship now? Is it the old one or the new one? Neither? At one point did it change over?

Here we see the result of the classic Greek atomistic mindset turned on human identity itself. We are invited to imagine that we ourselves are the ship. In a (gruesome) parallel, at what point would you lose your identity if a psychopathic murderer decided to whittle you down to nothing, removing parts of you piece by piece? (Unlike the ship, there would be the extra conundrum of whether you'd consider yourself to maintain your same identity after surely dying... but this is another path of questioning.)

Theseus' ship has all the hallmarks of a great thought experiment: it's simple but runs deep. What can it teach us about not just ourselves (i.e. the topic under investigation), but also the way in which we seek to answer these questions (indirectly also teaching us about ourselves!)? This thought experiment is great because it allows you to outline a set of possible answers, and examine the implications of each.

Firstly, you could potentially answer that the very moment you take a piece off the ship, you change it fundamentally, and it becomes a different ship. But if you wanted to say this, you'd have to concede that small atoms and molecules are constantly shifting into and out of the whole, with the result that the ship (or person) is never actually a static being with a fixed identity.

To the ancient Greeks, this was a ludicrous outcome and meant to be seen as paradoxical, but this viewpoint ("a man never steps in the same river twice") is not inconsistent with what we know about the world. We are reminded of the Eleatic school's single Being moving and shifting constantly—not a mathematical entity but an organic, organismic one.

A second potential answer is that the ship is more an idea than just the individual parts that make it up, and if you remove or replace parts, it's still the same ship. This leads you somewhat down the path of Plato's Forms (i.e. things are not merely objects in the material world, but abstract concepts, of which the physical is merely an instance).

Even if you replaced every wooden piece with an aluminium piece, say, the ship would still be the same ship. This view seems to hold that identity is more about a convention or deliberate attempt to group a collection of parts into a whole—it's not merely the existence of the parts, but the idea behind them, the organizing principle, structure, form or blueprint. If we demolish you completely but rebuild you using the code in your DNA, it's still *you*.

Others might say that identity is a question of continuity over time, and that the ship is whatever we've come to understand the ship as over time. The parts can change, the form can change, but if we keep on interacting with the ship as the ship, it *is* the ship, however it alters over time.

How can we use this thought experiment to improve or illuminate our own thinking about our own identities? Well, we can use it as a diagnostic—we all have beliefs and conceptions about ourselves and our place in the world, but they're often completely unexamined, habitual, or merely inherited from family or the culture we live in. Take the time now to consider your own perspective. With Theseus' ship in mind, answer the question: What makes you *you*? What part, when removed, makes you cease to be you?

Is it your physical traits (your race, sex, age, physical features, species)?

Is it your DNA, the idea of you as a whole?

Is it the history you've already lived with that identity?

Is it something somehow inside or because of your traits and structure, something like a soul, a personality, a string of thoughts (one level deeper than a blueprint)?

Or perhaps is there no such thing as a ship, no such thing as a person, and the boundaries we've decided exist between separate structures are really for convenience, but don't actually describe the world as it is?

Companies, musical groups, families, sports teams and the like can all change their constituent parts, yet still retain the same identity. All of us would say that an acorn, a fully grown oak tree and a pile of oak timber all share an identity, albeit at different life stages. As this example indicates, time is an important consideration. And even though most people would agree that cutting their hair doesn't drastically change who they are as a person, they almost certainly will say that they are a different person than they were ten or twenty years ago.

This thought experiment doesn't confront us with paradoxes so much as invite us to consider our working beliefs and mental models, and explore the implications they have. It teaches us to be explicit and deliberate in the thoughts we have, looking at what we believe rather than just believing it out of habit or convention. Exploring alternative answers (even counterintuitive ones) gives us a chance to more thoroughly evaluate the realm of possibilities—and perhaps adopt a mental perspective that is more accurate or more useful to us.

Follow this train of thought and you may find yourself benefitting in a spiritual, behavioral or psychological sense. For example, if each of your atoms and cells turns over many times every number of years, what's to say you can't be a completely different person after that time has elapsed? That would be inspiring, from a personal development standpoint.

On the other hand, if you are you no matter what, you literally could lose all your limbs, get total amnesia and undergo a full blood transfusion, and still you would not be able to shift your permanent identity.

Perhaps you only believe that some traits are essential (like race or species) whereas others are more malleable (like sex or gender—look closely at any debate around transgendered people and you will see clear echoes of Theseus' core argument, on both sides). All potential perspectives here are valid; the question is, which one will best serve your purposes?

Every day, you may go around the world with an *implicit* understanding of who you are as a human being. It's not explicit—you never deliberately and consciously decided to think this way, it merely happened, and continues to happen so long as you never question or examine it.

The issue is, your conception of who you are dramatically influences every aspect of your life—the only difference is whether you're doing it consciously or unconsciously. If you never give yourself the chance to question and revamp any unhelpful beliefs and attitudes, you're doomed to live with them and the limitations they bring.

The Man from the Swamp

A similar thought experiment spurs the same style of thinking using a different metaphor. Donald Davidson's "swamp man" is also about identity. It goes like this: a man is traveling through a swamp and is struck dead by lightning. At the very same instant the lighting also strikes the molecules in the swamp and rearranges them into an exact physical replica of the man, who then continues to live the first man's life (did we mention how painfully contrived thought experiments can sometimes be?)

The question is about the nature of the swamp man's *mind*. What kind of mind would he have, given that everything about him is physically the same as the first man? Davidson claimed that the swamp man would not actually be a person, since he would have no history and no memory; he is not a *genuine* being and anything he said would have no real meaning. He would appear to be interacting in all the normal ways, but he has no "causal history" and nothing to remember, since he never experienced it in the first place. He is just something that rose from the swamp and happens to resemble you...in every single way. But does that mean that you are nothing but your physical manifestation? No, probably not.

This is akin to saying that a new ship built out of bits and pieces of the old ship is not really the old ship, since it has no sense of history, context or continuity. Even if all the parts are the same, the first ship might have had a long history that the new one simply lacks. Does that mean that we are only our experiences and neuronal connections? No, probably not.

This swamp man looks like you, is conscious, and for all intents and purposes is you on a physical level. But is he you?

We can understand the swamp man as something of an addendum to Theseus' ship, which acts as evidence that the identity of a whole is so much more than its components. It's essentially asking what happens to the ship's personality, history, memory and experience. With inanimate objects, we tend to think in terms of structure, function and components. But with humans, we are clearly made of more than our physical parts, which the swamp man experiment shows quite clearly.

In fact, this train of thought makes it quite obvious what we consider to be our identity—t's not about our bodies, it's about our personalities, experiences, and patterns of thought. If we cut out our brains and put them into host bodies, we would probably still consider that organism to be *us*.

What this thought experiment teaches us is to whittle down our suppositions and theories to really arrive at what we believe, what we claim, and what we assume. This thought experiment is like a refinement of Theseus' ship, acting like a scalpel to further narrow down the question: What is a person?

Beam Me Up, Scotty

A simpler version is to ask whether the people who go through the "transporter" in

Star Trek (dissembled and reassembled on an atomic level) are still the same people or entirely new, different ones. The difference here is that the person is somehow transported with all their memories and ideas intact. Would you consider the swamp man fundamentally different from a person that has gone through a transporter? (A related question—how on earth could a transporter transport people's memory and experience? Where are they, if not in the cells and atoms of the body?)

This thought experiment is also called "Parfit's transporter" (sci-fi and speculative philosophy are close friends with a long and tangled history). It doesn't matter that transporters aren't real—yet. The creators of Google have frequently claimed they were inspired by *Star Trek*'s gadgetry, as though sci-fi paved the way for regular sci to follow. What matters is what they can show us.

Asking these questions allows us to have more robust and sophisticated answers to questions like what happens to "us" after we die, whether we'd be the same people following a coma or traumatic brain injury, or whether we're going to be the same people at the end of life as we were at the beginning.

When you chew over these questions long enough, you start to see that the question of identity is one of continuity from the past to now—of something that persists despite change and movement through this thing we call time. Thought experiments can help us better understand this continuity, what it is and isn't.

You might decide that identity is a bodily phenomenon, a question of continuity of the literal parts making up an entity. Then you would be faced with certain consequences: that at some point you didn't have an identity, and you will cease to have one at some point, too (i.e. after your parts disassemble and you die.)

You might instead say that continuity in soul or spirit constitutes identity. But then you would have to figure out exactly what this invisible, intangible substance really was, that somehow inhabited the physical form—and there are problems with this too, to say the least!

You could say that continuous identity is about stable patterns of behavior and personality, and that the emergent properties of your constituent parts acting as a whole are what amounts to your personality. But even people who believe this still make room for the fact that personalities, beliefs and ideas still do change, leaving us back at square one.

You could say that the idea of identity is itself a falsehood, or a trick of language, a little like you could argue that inches, degrees Celsius or the border of Mexico don't really exist, we merely behave as if they do.

The question here is not which perspective is correct, but rather to give ourselves the chance to explore the consequences of adopting one or the other viewpoint. If you behaved as though you were a collection of physical parts animated by a spirit that persisted after your physical body died, you might take different risks, interpret life events differently, have different goals, deal with adversity differently, seek out a different occupation, and fear different things. In short, the way you think about yourself has the most profound of implications—it draws the limits and bounds of how you live.

Knowing what you know about Theseus' ship, about the transporter analogies or the swamp man story, what would you like to use going forward, and why? Practice a little deliberate, conscious self-determination and try on the thoughts and mental schemes that you wish to inhabit, rather than merely occupying whatever model you've found yourself in by habit or accident.

Thought experiments like this can seem pointless or unconnected to any real-world phenomena, but they are more ubiquitous than you think. Take a look at the following questions, and ask yourself what your answers tell you about your working models and beliefs:

- Where does life begin? It could be at conception, at the first detectable heartbeat, or the moment a baby is born.

But then, when is a baby a full human being? When does it have personhood— is this something it was born with, or will it grow into it?

- On the other end of life, when does a person officially die, in your opinion? It may be once they stop breathing, thinking or having a heartbeat. But why these signs of life and not others?
- Do people have souls? What about personalities? Is there any difference between a soul and a personality, and if so, what is it?
- Can people fundamentally change who they are?
- Have you changed since this morning? What about over the course of a week, month or year? What does all this say about the potential for personal development?

If someone experienced a traumatic event, the trauma essentially follows them precisely because they feel as though they are the same person as the one who experienced the trauma. The event is passed. What carries into the present, however, is the *identity* the person retains of being a victim or survivor.

As a practical example of how identity thought experiments can enrich our world, consider two people who have undergone a trauma. One conceives of their identity as fluid, up for negotiation, and constantly evolving. The other sees themselves as fixed and non-negotiable. After a trauma, the former is more likely to say, "I've moved on; I'm a different person now" while the latter is more likely to say, "I'll always be a victim of such-and-such injustice and nothing I can do can change that. It's who I am."

Thinking deliberately of identity also gives you the chance to enter into a "growth mindset"—i.e., conducting yourself as though you can always learn, develop and change. This means you can admit when you're wrong and actually improve, which is much harder to do if you sincerely believe your personality is fixed and spells a destiny that you can never really change. Depending on how you answered the questions above, your self-belief could pave the way for freedom or apathy, for being proactive or passive, resigned or open-minded and curious. Isn't it true that people only live within the limits they first set for themselves?

The way you think about yourself affects how you process risk, adversity or opportunity. It tells you how to interpret your experience, how to plan for the future, how to talk about the past. There are arguably as many ways of conceiving of the self as there are selves.

The question is, which way of thinking about yourself offers you the most control, optimism, understanding, beauty, insight? Which one feels best? Makes the most sense? Matches with the world you actually perceive in front of you? Is there perhaps another way of conceiving of the entire endeavor that strikes you as preferable? These are all realms of questioning you might not have explored without the original poke from a few seemingly silly thought experiments!

Takeaways:

- Existence and identity are deep topics. One is reminded of Descartes' immortal declaration of "I think, therefore I am." In a way, that's where we are headed in this chapter. The concept of personal identity makes you confront how you choose to define it, and also forces you to think about how you choose to define yourself.

- We start with the thought experiment of Theseus' Ship, which asks you to evaluate at which point a ship is still that same ship if you continually remove its components, and even more so if you remove the components and then replace them with entirely different ones. So it forces you to consider what you use to construct an identity. Is it just the individual components? Is there something about a ship that can be more than the sum of its parts? And what about us—what makes us a particular person, and if removed from our physical body, what would we then become?

- Each of the thought experiments in this chapter follows the same line of thought.

Swamp man asks how you would evaluate the identity of a swamp monster that rises after you are struck dead by lightning. This monster is physically the same as you, down to the molecule. And yet, it doesn't have your personality, experiences, or quirks. Is it you? It seems to be a clear no; but what if this swamp monster also retains all of your memories and experiences? This possibility becomes much hazier, yet it's still clear that we consider the identity of living beings to be far more than a simple physical representation.

- Finally, Parfit's Transporter asks how we would feel if we were physically torn apart, and then reassembled every time we used a transporter, as in the fictional sci-fi television show *Star Trek*. Are you still you, even though the previous version of you is for all intents and purposes torn to shreds? Is this newly reformed being you, simply because it possesses your experiences and memories?

- When you chew over these questions long enough, you start to see that the question of identity is one of continuity from the past to the present—of something that persists despite change and movement through this thing we call time. Body parts, soul/spirit/personality, and behavior/personality are all part of the equation. The question here is not which perspective is correct, but rather to give ourselves the chance to explore the consequences of adopting one or the other viewpoint. The way you think about yourself has the most profound of implications—it draws the limits and bounds of how you live.

Chapter 5. The Nature of Perception

Our final chapter, in a way, brings us to the heart of the deepest value of thought experiment: as a sneaky way to delve into how we perceive the world, and why. This is the realm of what philosophers call *theory of mind*. Through what channels do we experience the world, and are we (*can we be*) accurate in our assessment? The thought experiments below attempt to unpack some of these themes by looking closely at what it takes to dismantle all the ordinary perceptive abilities we take for granted (i.e. the ones you've been using all along in reading this book). While they're not wrong or even necessarily lacking, they can always stand to improve, especially when you take a look at the ways your perception can be bent.

While our first chapter was about what can be known and learnt, and the limits of our knowledge, we go a little further in this chapter to try and understand perception, experience and being in and of itself.

As your eyes scan along the letters on this page, a million separate processes are happening. It seems like such a simple thing: to see what you see, to think what you think. But by slowing everything down and taking a microscopic view on things we ordinarily take for granted, we open up new worlds of insight—for example, the entirely new universe of what *other peoples'* experience are like compared to our own.

As with all thought experiments, the right kind of question can offer you insights far more valuable than merely having an answer to your question.

Do You Speak Chinese?

Right now, complex questions that arise from developments in machine learning and artificial intelligence have us reflexively questioning our own human limits where language, experience and knowledge are concerned. The "Chinese room" is a thought experiment that simply but powerfully illustrates the heart of the matter. John Searle created this experiment in 1980 to explain why machines or computers don't and can never be said to be intelligent, or think in the same sense that we do.

Now, it's important to understand exactly what is meant here by AI. Some machines behave "as if" they were intelligent but are merely simulating thought or going through the motions. Others are more sophisticated and can be said to actually comprehend things, i.e. not just something that acts like a mind, but is one. Searle was talking about the latter type when he proposed the Chinese room thought experiment.

It goes like this. You are an English speaker who knows no other language, locked in a room with some Chinese writing, a second set of writing and some rules, written in English, for matching up the first batch of Chinese with the second. Just by looking at the shape of the Chinese characters, you can see which group of symbols corresponds to which other group.

So far so good. You are also given a third set of Chinese writing and still more instructions (again in English) that let you draw correlations between the third batch and the first two. The first batch is called a script, the second a story and the third are called questions. However, you are not told any of this. You are asked only to provide responses, called answers to the questions.

It takes you a while to learn the rules. Despite not knowing a word of Chinese, you eventually become so good at supplying the right answers to the questions that, to someone looking from the outside in, you appear to be fluent in Chinese.

So, what are you really doing by manipulating the symbols in this way? Searle would say you are behaving as a computer would, and even though your behavior is indistinguishable from a Chinese speaker, you are not one. You are merely applying a script to process a story and respond in the form of answers. You don't even strictly need to know that these are "questions" or "answers" to respond correctly.

The inputs and outputs are the same as the process for a real Chinese speaker, but what is missing is comprehension. According to Searle, this situation is analogous to what a computer does—it behaves in all the ways to *simulate* thinking, yet does not really do any thinking, since it has no real understanding of what it is doing. The computer is simply manipulating symbols. For Searle, it didn't matter how complex the behavior, set of rules or symbols; if there's no understanding, there's no actual thought.

Philosophers call this symbol juggling "syntax," but the meaning ascribed to those symbols is "semantics." So, although a machine can demonstrate syntactical behavior, it doesn't have semantics and lacks any kind of mind as we understand it. A machine can "say" something like, "the sky is blue" without having any eyes to see the color blue, any feelings about the fact, any past history with skies or anything else. It has no beliefs, feelings, or indeed any interior life that we typically associate with having a mind.

Now, we won't take the time to dwell here on AI as a topic, as enormous and interesting a field as it is. Rather, we can use some of these ideas to springboard a more general inquiry into how we understand and perceive our world, how we acquire knowledge, and what we do with it when we have it. You might have had a few responses to hearing about the Chinese room. For example, how do we know that a Chinese speaker really is a Chinese speaker?

Well, simple: by their external behavior. It's all that we can see, observe, or know. If this is enough to convince us another person is a Chinese speaker, why do we have more stringent standards for machines? In fact, one could argue (if one was feeling argumentative) that we don't have much proof that we're *not* doing this when we claim to be able to speak a language!

There are many responses and counterarguments to Searle's hypothetical situation, most of which are concerned more technically with linguistics, cognitive science, programming, consciousness and artificial intelligence. However, thought experiments allow us to engage with these questions without necessarily needing a deep understanding of the technical details.

We can ask what this experiment shows us not about AI, but about ourselves. If we say that a machine can't have a mind, well, why not exactly? More precisely, what is it about what we do that makes us distinct from a robot programmed to do the same thing?

Where exactly do things like "intention," "consciousness" or "understanding" actually come from, and why is a mere replica of these things not the same as the original? You may be seeing parallels here with the swamp man, as well as the shadows on Plato's cave. In fact, you may start to see the bigger question: real consciousness versus a symbol, illusion or image of consciousness.

Though these thought experiments appear to be about computers, they are really about humans, and they're what we're really talking about when we say we have *minds.* The computational theory of mind says that mental states are like the software installed on the hardware of our physical brains. Mental states are then characterized by whatever function you're performing at the time. If we accept this model, we have to concede that computers can do the same, and that AI can think in the same way we can, only with hardware that is slightly different.

Alan Turing's famous test for machine intelligence was whether a machine could converse with a human in so authentic a way that the human would not realize it was talking to a machine. Searle saw the human mind as more than just a program, and would disagree that the Turing test shows us anything about the "mind" of a machine.

Isn't a mind so much more than having an intelligent conversation? More than just being able to juggle symbols? What about the feelings of love, the ability to dream, to have a sensation of consciousness, to really smell the proverbial roses, to believe deeply in the experience that you are alive and have a distinct being?

These questions bring us to a final consideration: how accessible is the idea of the "mind" anyway?

What are we really talking about, and are we even talking about the same thing? Let's zoom right out again and, as we've learnt in previous thought experiments, take a closer look at all the assumptions we've made in constructing the Chinese room argument.

A related thought experiment is the antepenultimate one we'll consider in this book, and in a way the most fundamental. Wittgenstein was a philosopher who wanted to cut to the heart of all philosophical questions by looking closely at the *way* in which we connect our thoughts and ideas about the world with the world itself. He was interested in language and logic—not the content of an argument, but its underlying mechanism.

What's a Beetle?

Throughout this book, words and symbols have been used to evoke memories, linguistic conventions, allegories and metaphors to *point to* various aspects of the world, and summon a particular response in the reader—you. In a way, it's a game of broken telephone, with the message potentially altered in each step along the chain of communication: How can the author of any book be sure that the reader truly comprehends what's been said?

Much like the Chinese room problem, he may offer some response that looks *as if* he understands and comprehends the information in a certain way, but then, to perceive him doing so would entail passing his response through the lens of your own experience. At some point, we need to look at the world without symbols. Can we? And for that matter, even if we can't, does it ultimately matter?

Wittgenstein suggested a "beetle in a box" analogy to make clear this fundamental difficulty. This thought experiment says a lot about the queries we've already engaged with (some of it not particularly flattering!).

Here it is: picture that everyone in the world has a box with a beetle inside it. Nobody is allowed to see into anyone else's box, only their own. However, we're all free to talk about what's in our box—i.e., to use symbol and language to refer to it. People may eventually decide together that we all have a "beetle" in our box, and for all intents and purposes we would then start to assume that we all had the same thing. The word would eventually come to represent whatever-it-is-in-the-box, but we may forget that *we never actually see into someone else's box.*

The analogy is obvious: the box is each individual mind, the beetle is the mysterious and ineffable contents of that mind, and the fact that other peoples' boxes are hidden from us is the idea that we never truly have access to another being's mind. Yes, we may have plenty of words, ideas, symbols, concepts, analogies etc. to refer to the beetle, but the fact remains: we never see it directly. Indeed, if the boxes could all be opened one day there's no reason to expect that the same thing should jump out of everyone's box.

It's a staggering assumption, and one that really makes other philosophical inquiry look a bit puny: the idea that everyone else's mind works like ours, and that their experiences are comparable to ours. The more you think about it, the more potential you can see for another being's experience of life being so fundamentally different and alien from yours as to seem incomprehensible, even though on the surface we are sharing some common linguistic conventions to deal with each other.

Taking it further, Wittgenstein suggests that it doesn't even really matter what's in the box—we will never know. Does this mean, then, that "beetle" simply means "this thing I have in my box, whatever it is"? This has some subtle yet profound implications. The "mind" is then simply "what each person feels their mind to be."

It's a sobering thought: our deepest experiences and perceptions are fundamentally closed off to others, and permanently private. All we have recourse to is language, or the rules of language—

much like we do in the Chinese room. You can see, then, the implied problem: how do we *know* whether someone is really intelligent, whether they've understood something, whether their experience of "sad" or "orange" or "totalitarian" or even "being" is the same as yours? However, a consolation should be that we are all blind to each other's boxes, and either converge enough, or function well enough to exist in the world together without this seemingly important piece of information.

Wittgenstein had trouble conveying his message, and was frequently misunderstood himself. He claimed, for example, that we can't necessarily know that there is a thing called a mind in the first place. Sure, we all use *words* like "mind," and this word, as part of a shared language, has a meaning that we've all used in the real world.

However, Wittgenstein was careful to suggest that that was it—we could not make any further claims about what was in the box, i.e. what our minds actually were, since we could never measure, compare or confirm its existence.

All we can ever do is to see into our own minds (maybe?) and describe the experience in words to other people, and vice versa. This language we use necessarily has to be shared with others; you cannot have your own personal language to describe your own personal experience. If you've ever tried to verbalize a very personal event—a strange dream, a mystical experience, an impression, an intuition or a deep emotional sensation— you may already know how hopeless it can feel to ever capture it properly in words.

And even if you did, there's absolutely no guarantee that the person hearing it wouldn't misinterpret your description or add their own flavor to it. So, instead of looking closely at the beetles, at the box, at what we can learn from each other about beetles and so on, we can press a little further and become conscious of the relationship between what's in the box and the words we use for it.

As with every other thought experiment so far, let's give ourselves a moment to think about what Wittgenstein's beetles-in-a-box situation tells us about ourselves, the world, language and our minds. By thinking through the paths Wittgenstein invites us down, we are training our brains, as with other thought experiments, to look not *within* the realms of our own cognitive and linguistic boundaries, but *beyond* them, and to the boundaries themselves. We learn to get comfortable asking questions about our questions, talking about our words, thinking about our thoughts. Congratulations, you're now a philosopher!

On a very superficial level, this exercise can help us recognize instances where we have merely assumed that other people have the same definitions as us and use language in exactly the same way. How many miscommunications could be avoided in relationships or work situations if people took the time to clarify what each meant when they used certain words? For example, do both people in a relationship agree on what "cheating" refers to? Does every politician have the same idea of what "living wage" actually means?

It's true that clarifying differences in definitions for words is merely an exercise in better aligning the language we use—we still don't know what's in another person's mind. However, many people incorrectly assume as a given that we are all on the same page language-wise, and never stop to think whether disagreement or misunderstanding is not conceptual, but merely a question of unacknowledged differences, maybe due to culture, personal history or simply personality.

But Wittgenstein also makes us consider something a bit more profound. How shall we conduct ourselves knowing that there are simply realms of private experience that are *never accessible to us, ever*? You've probably heard people say things like, "Don't judge others, you don't know what they've been through." They're right. We can see people's behavior, and hear the words they speak. But we will never know how much pain they are in, what love feels like from inside their heads, or indeed what they think and feel when they see you!

Perhaps understanding this is a path to real compassion for other people, and ourselves. If someone tells us about their experience, all we can ever do is believe them and trust that their account is "real." We can never tell anyone else's story for them—each of us is the ultimate arbiter of our own reality. In this way, people who've survived abuse or war or natural disaster can sometimes find empowerment by owning their own experiences; not seeing themselves through the lens of someone else's understanding, but defining their own experience on their own terms. At the end of the day, all any of us really have is our experience, as it is, right here in our own minds.

This book has spoken at length about how human beings use symbols, what language is, how logic works, and how we can get a better grip on it all. What a marvelous puzzle it all is!

Somehow, though, Wittgenstein pressed the matter to its final conclusion and brought much of philosophy into a quiet inner place.

No matter the abstractions, words, ideas, logic or clever cognitive tricks, no matter the technological developments or scientific advances, at the end of it all we are still here, living and breathing entities in the concrete world, quite profoundly alone with our own ineffable and private, limited worlds, inside our literal skulls.

What is it like to be you? How is it to be somebody else? Engaging with the previous thought experiments arguably helped you develop all the bells and whistles of your own metacognition, turning a curious eye onto your own seeing. But this final thought experiment invites us to grapple with the very ground of our lived experience, our consciousness itself.

A Tale of Fish

We end this book not with a thought experiment per se, but with a philosophical stroll into perception and how we are all left holding our own boxes of beetles, in a manner of speaking. Despite our best efforts, we are necessarily limited in our perception. And though it doesn't need to be stated again, this should inform how we approach problem-solving, decisions, relationships, and any other life situation that demands analysis.

If nothing else, the takeaway from this book should be that the more you think you know, the less you truly do. The parable of the happiness of fish wraps up this chapter and book neatly with a bow.

This parable comes courtesy of Zhuangzi, the same Taoist philosopher who posed the butterfly dream question earlier. The following is attributed to *Zhuangzi: The Essential Writings with Selections from Traditional Commentaries* by Brook Ziporyn.

> Zhuangzi and Huizi were strolling along the bridge over the Hao River. Zhuangzi said, "The minnows swim about so freely, following the openings wherever they take them. Such is the happiness of fish."
>
> Huizi said, "You are not a fish, so whence do you know the happiness of fish?"

Zhuangzi said, "You are not I, so whence do you know I don't know the happiness of fish?"

Huizi said, "I am not you, to be sure, so I don't know what it is to be you. But by the same token, since you are certainly not a fish, my point about your inability to know the happiness of fish stands intact."

Zhuangzi said, "Let's go back to the starting point. You said, 'Whence do you know the happiness of fish?' Since your question was premised on your knowing that I know it, I must have known it from here, up above the Hao River."

This exchange between Zhuangzi and Huizi seems circular and redundant, but what is being demonstrated here?

No one can peer into the minds of others—and this is shown right from the outset in two ways. Zhuangzi first assets that he knows the happiness of the fish, but in fact, he is not presupposing to know their state of mind, only that fish are simply doing what fish do, and this is their happiness. It's that simple. Zhuangzi knows the happiness of fish because fish do what fish do and he can see them doing it.

There is already a misunderstanding here due to different perspectives and mindsets, as Huizi won't tolerate this line of thinking and assumes that Zhuangzi can inhabit the minds of those very fish to understand their emotional state of mind. This is the first way that we see different perspectives being pointed out in a manner that we probably erroneously employ in our everyday lives.

And second, Huizi points out that Zhuangzi is not a fish, so how could he possibly know what brings them happiness, just as the two of them cannot possibly know what the other knows or does not know. If Zhuangzi cannot know the happiness of fish because he is not a fish, then, applying the same reasoning, Huizi cannot know whether Zhuangzi knows it or not. If the first premise is correct, then this conclusion would certainly seem to logically follow.

Perhaps it all is but a dream, or a dream within a dream. Zhuangzi "knows" the happiness of fish just as any dreamer "knows" the content of his dream, and this works equally well for the dreaming or ostensibly awake. And in either case, whether dreaming or awake, it does not matter, for it is the experience which has arisen.

We don't know what other people are really *saying*, because it's always tainted with their own perspectives, and we can't read their minds. We don't really know what other people are *thinking* because we are not them. We don't always know what we *ourselves* are thinking because we're constantly influenced by the people and circumstances around us.

And in the end, maybe it's all a dream, and we're just a butterfly waking up from a deep nap in mid-spring.

As we end this book, we find ourselves right back where we started—with questions. Having taken your mind out to visit distant arenas of possibility, you've given your brain exercise, so it can engage with even bigger, subtler, more mind-boggling problems the next time round. You'll teach yourself to watch for your assumptions, and question them often and rigorously. You'll condition yourself to tolerate uncertainty and be OK with suspending judgment rather than accepting conclusions on incomplete information.

You'll frequently examine not just the content of your thought, but the architecture holding it all together. You won't care about being right—and might end up being right more often as a result! You'll become curious about *how* you're thinking, or even why.

Just as plenty of exercise makes a body robust and healthy, regularly putting your mind through the works develops robust and healthy cognitive abilities and, if you're like Wittgenstein, it may even kindle the sentiment of life being filled with something poetic and truly ineffable. What else is your mind, after all, but an organ through which to experience wonder at being alive, here in this strange and boundless place we call the world?

Takeaways:

- Perception is necessarily unique and individual, because our perception is not just a shared circumstance or setting. Perception comes through the total sum of our experiences, memories, feelings, emotions, upbringings, and more. When phrased thusly, it seems an exercise in obviousness to say that our perceptions are all different. But that's just the tip of the iceberg in thinking about the concept of perception—how we understand the world around us.
- We start with the thought experiment of the Chinese room, wherein language is reduced to a series of inputs and appropriate outputs. You are sitting in a room, and you are trained to recognize Chinese characters shown to you, and then display an appropriate response. For all intents and purposes, anyone

outside the room interacting with you would assume that you are a native Chinese speaker—but you're just pushing buttons. So what is language? It's about understanding, emotion, and empathy; yet what happens if we conceive of it as a calculator with numbers and equations? What does it mean to actually understand someone on a real level, instead of just responding to them as you think you should? For all of our best intentions, are we just simulating thinking, behavior, actions, and emotion?

- Perception can also be shown to be wholly unimportant in the grand scheme of things, as demonstrated by Wittgenstein's beetle in a box thought experiment. Suppose we have a box of objects that we call beetles, and so does everyone else. The thing is, no one can ever look inside each other's boxes, so it's a total mystery as to what a beetle means to all of us. The analogy is obvious: the box is each individual mind, the beetle is the mysterious and ineffable contents of that mind, and the fact that other peoples' boxes are hidden from us is the idea that we never truly have access to another being's mind. The way we perceive a simple beetle, and extrapolating to how we see the world, is singular. We can guess, and we can assume, but our deepest experiences and perceptions are fundamentally closed off to others, and permanently private.

- We end the book right back where we start—with questions. And this is illustrated through the parable of the happiness of fish, as noted by Chinese philosopher Zhuangzi. No one can peer into the minds of others—and this is shown right from the outset in two ways. Zhuangzi first assets that he knows the happiness of the fish, but in fact, he is not presupposing to know their state of mind, only that fish are simply doing what fish do, and this is their happiness. It's that simple. Zhuangzi knows the happiness of fish because fish do what fish do and he can see them doing it. However, Huizi points out that Zhuangzi is not a fish, so how could he possibly know what brings them happiness, just as the two of them cannot possibly know what the other knows or does not know. If Zhuangzi cannot know the happiness of fish because he is not a fish, then, applying the same reasoning, Huizi cannot know whether Zhuangzi knows it or not. If the first premise is correct, then this conclusion would certainly seem to logically follow. And in the end, maybe it's all a dream, and we're just a butterfly waking up from a deep nap in mid-spring.

Summary Guide

Chapter 1. Thinking About Thinking

- A thought experiment is much more than a "what if" scenario played out to its logical or philosophical end. It's a grand arena where you can take your brain out to learn, explore, grow, and play. It's how you can truly learn to think and conceive of the world outside of your own perspective. Some thought experiments will force you to expand your mind in certain ways, while others will encourage you to utilize novel perspectives and lines of thought. Using thought experiments in your own life will make you a more focused, more robust thinker with a cognitive and intellectual scope far wider than if you'd never challenged yourself in this particular way. Learn to search for an answer, even when there is no true correct or wrong way of thinking. Stretch your thinking capabilities and boundaries and see how things look afterwards.

141

- A prime example of mulling around solutions and perspectives for which a million variables exist is the Trolley Problem. Would you rather allow one person to die or five? This is a classic thought experiment that forces you into a series of escalating moral dilemmas. It makes you consider who you are, and what you value, and why that is. In the end, nothing is solved or clarified, except your own thoughts. There is no answer except to systematically learn and explore.

- More practical applications of thought experiments come in the form of Schrodinger's cat (molecular structure), Albert Einstein's riding a wave (relativity and the speed of light), and Newton's Cannon (gravity and orbits). These theories mostly concerned hard sciences, and explored them in a way that was impossible at the time (and still is currently). Today, we might have computers to map out simulations and projections, but thought experiments are still able to touch the unknown and the unquantifiable.

- Get comfortable thinking about thinking, because that's what we'll be doing throughout the book. The thought experiments we'll be exploring in this book have all served a particular purpose in their historical context. However, in learning about them, we achieve the broader goal of teaching ourselves to reach outside our own habitual thoughts and beliefs.

Chapter 2. The Nature of Uncertainty

- Uncertainty is a very uncomfortable concept to wrap our minds around. The human brain highly prefers a concrete answer, thought, or even guess. It's why we jump to conclusions and prioritize speed over accuracy. Learning to thrive in the limbo of uncertainty can greatly benefit your thinking skills because it teaches you to slow down, check your assumptions, put away your ego, and embrace the ultimate version of "I have no idea." Once you can accept this starting point, the world will suddenly open up—because you are listening and observing.

- We kick the chapter off with a thought experiment dubbed Plato's Cave. It tells the tale of prisoners shackled in a dark cave facing inside, so the only thing they can see is a series of shadows from people, animals, and events going on outside. Of course, this is not the real world—from our vantage point. But to them, these shadows are everything, and it is unthinkable that anything else exists. So the question comes—how can we ever know if what we are seeing is merely a shadow, or the true form and nature of the thing? Of people? Of ourselves? Accept that perception is necessarily flawed, and attempt to think from the ground up.

- Next, we delve into a thought experiment that you are already familiar with. It's called the brain in a vat experiment, and it closely mirrors (or rather, the other way around) the premise for the movie *The Matrix.* What if we are all indeed just brains in vats of liquid, being externally fed a lifetime of experiences and nutrients? How could we ever know the difference unless we were physically shown the jar? And then how could we know that this vision was also true and unfiltered and untampered with? We can't. And that's the point. There's more uncertainty, even to our very nature, and we again should cease all assumptions and think and question more thoroughly.

- Next, we have Descartes' demon problem. This can be said to go a step farther, as it assumes that it's possible (a non-zero chance, to be sure) that a demon is possessing you and causing you to reason and analyze incorrectly or unreliably. Thus? We can't trust ourselves. We can only look at evidence and build from there.

- Finally, we come to a short parable and thought experiment that Chinese philosopher Zhuangzi put forth: the butterfly dream. If Zhuangzi dreamt that he was a butterfly, and his dream seemed so genuine as to be reality, who's to say that in his current life as a human, he is not just a butterfly dreaming that he is here? And again, how can we ever be sure, even about our very existence? You already know the answer, and how that should affect your approach to thinking.

Chapter 3. The Nature of the Infinite

- The infinite is one of the most confusing concepts to grasp. The truth is, in reality, things beyond a certain point of frequency or amount (even money) cease to hold any meaning for us. We just can't imagine or visualize them, and thus they become meaningless. And yet, playing with this concept and understanding it a little better will help stretch your thinking and expand your mind. Taking a subject out of the ether and examining it in a reality-based and consequential way can help you extract a few lessons on extremely big, and extremely small, probabilities, and understand why a mathematical construct like 1/3 cannot truly be expressed as a decimal.

- Any discussion of the infinite must begin with the thought experiment of Lucretius' spear. If you contend that the universe if infinite, and then you walk right up to the edge (first of all, what would the edge even constitute), and then you throw a javelin, then what would happen? Would it bounce off something? Would it disappear? Would it just keep sailing because the universe is indeed infinite? What exactly would take place? Thinking through this abstraction makes clear that we have to suspend reality sometimes and redefine what we think is possible. You might even find that you have been asking wrong questions all along by not accounting for what you didn't consider.
- The infinite monkey theorem is just that—what happens when you put an infinite amount of monkeys into a room with typewriters? Well, the law of big numbers and probabilities dictate that eventually, they will produce a word for word script of any of Shakespeare's plays. In truth, this is a nod to how anything is possible with enough inputs,

and conversely, nothing is impossible with enough inputs. You can't rule out anything that has a slight possibility or chance, and you must always account for everything that is possible. Something is possible from almost nothing. It doesn't sound like a revelation, but it's a more eloquent way of encouraging thoroughness and looking at the concept of randomness and serendipity.

- Finally, what's half of half? 25 percent. What's half of that? 12.5 percent. What happens when you get to infinitesimal numbers? Do you ever reach zero? Nope. But is that reflective of reality? Nope. That's what Zeno's paradoxes sought to explain: what seems to be apparent and obvious on paper often has no bearing to reality. Once again, the map is not the territory. Zeno's paradoxes play out at the interface between math and life, between concept and reality. Importantly, they may show us how uncomfortable the fit really is: what can seem "intuitively" correct can be shown to be completely wrong mathematically, statistically or theoretically. Could it be that the conception of "infinity" itself is flawed, and so every story based on it will eventually contain strange paradoxes like these?

Chapter 4. The Nature of Existence and Identity

- Existence and identity are deep topics. One is reminded of Descartes' immortal declaration of "I think, therefore I am." In a way, that's where we are headed in this chapter. The concept of personal identity makes you confront how you choose to define it, and also forces you to think about how you choose to define yourself.
- We start with the thought experiment of Theseus' Ship, which asks you to evaluate at which point a ship is still that same ship if you continually remove its components, and even more so if you remove the components and then replace them with entirely different ones. So it forces you to consider what you use to construct an identity. Is it just the individual components? Is there

something about a ship that can be more than the sum of its parts? And what about us—what makes us a particular person, and if removed from our physical body, what would we then become?

- Each of the thought experiments in this chapter follows the same line of thought. Swamp man asks how you would evaluate the identity of a swamp monster that rises after you are struck dead by lightning. This monster is physically the same as you, down to the molecule. And yet, it doesn't have your personality, experiences, or quirks. Is it you? It seems to be a clear no; but what if this swamp monster also retains all of your memories and experiences? This possibility becomes much hazier, yet it's still clear that we consider the identity of living beings to be far more than a simple physical representation.

- Finally, Parfit's Transporter asks how we would feel if we were physically torn apart, and then reassembled every time we used a transporter, as in the fictional sci-fi television show *Star Trek*. Are you still you, even though the previous version of you is for all intents and purposes torn to shreds? Is this newly reformed being you, simply because it possesses your experiences and memories?

- When you chew over these questions long enough, you start to see that the question of identity is one of continuity from the past to the present—of something that persists despite change and movement through this thing we call time. Body parts, soul/spirit/personality, and behavior/personality are all part of the equation. The question here is not which perspective is correct, but rather to give ourselves the chance to explore the consequences of adopting one or the other viewpoint. The way you think about yourself has the most profound of implications—it draws the limits and bounds of how you live.

Chapter 5. The Nature of Perception

- Perception is necessarily unique and individual, because our perception is not just a shared circumstance or setting. Perception comes through the total sum of our experiences, memories, feelings, emotions, upbringings, and more. When phrased thusly, it seems an exercise in obviousness to say that our perceptions are all different. But that's just the tip of the iceberg in thinking about the concept of perception—how we understand the world around us.

- We start with the thought experiment of the Chinese room, wherein language is reduced to a series of inputs and appropriate outputs. You are sitting in a room, and you are trained to recognize Chinese characters shown to you, and then display an appropriate response. For all intents and purposes, anyone outside the room interacting with you would assume that you are a native Chinese speaker—but you're just pushing buttons. So what is language? It's about understanding, emotion, and empathy; yet what happens if we conceive of it as a calculator with numbers and equations? What does it mean to actually understand someone on a real level, instead of just responding to them as you think you should? For all of our best intentions, are we just simulating thinking, behavior, actions, and emotion?

- Perception can also be shown to be wholly unimportant in the grand scheme of things, as demonstrated by Wittgenstein's beetle in a box thought experiment. Suppose we have a box of objects that we call beetles, and so does everyone else. The thing is, no one can ever look inside each other's boxes, so it's a total mystery as to what a beetle means to all of us. The analogy is obvious: the box is each individual mind, the beetle is the mysterious and ineffable contents of that mind, and the fact that other peoples' boxes are hidden from us is the idea that we never truly have access to another being's mind. The way we perceive a simple beetle, and extrapolating to how we see the world, is singular. We can guess, and we can assume, but our deepest experiences and perceptions are fundamentally closed off to others, and permanently private.

- We end the book right back where we start—with questions. And this is illustrated through the parable of the happiness of fish, as noted by Chinese philosopher Zhuangzi. No one can peer into the minds of others—and this is shown right from the outset in two ways. Zhuangzi first assets that he knows the happiness of the fish, but in fact, he is not presupposing to know their state of mind, only that fish are simply doing what fish do, and this is their happiness. It's that simple. Zhuangzi knows the happiness of fish because fish do what fish do and he can see them doing it. However, Huizi points out that Zhuangzi is not a fish, so how could he possibly know what brings them happiness, just as the two of them cannot possibly know what the other knows or does not know. If Zhuangzi cannot know the happiness of fish because he is not a fish, then, applying the same reasoning, Huizi cannot know whether Zhuangzi knows it or not. If the first premise is correct, then this conclusion would certainly seem to logically follow. And in the end, maybe it's all a dream, and we're just a butterfly waking up from a deep nap in mid-spring.